D0344150

Dressed to Kill

Contents

Acknowledgements

We should like to express our thanks to Steve Parton for his helpful suggestions and interest, and to the following who so readily gave us their advice and expertise when asked: Geoffrey Bucknall, Bob Church, Jim Clements, David Collyer, Gordon Fraser, John Goddard, Brian Harris, Roger Hurst, Sid Knight, Mike Peters, Taff Price, Jack Simpson, John Wadham and John Wilshaw.

We are also grateful to the following organisations for their help: Fishermen's Feathers, House of Hardy and Tom C. Saville.

The publishers wish to thank Charles Jardine for producing the excellent cover painting and also the line drawings that appear through the book.

Introduction

Any stillwater angler who is versatile and flexible in his approach to his fishing, and dresses his own flies to support his strategies, is likely to derive the maximum enjoyment and success from his sport.

Imitative and lure fishing are complementary arts for the successful stillwater fisherman to be used as and when appropriate. Our greatest love in trout fishing is to take trout on small imitative patterns in conjunction with a floating line, but if you are out on Rutland Water's 3400 acres, and shoals of rainbow trout are cruising ten to fifteen feet down sieving daphnia for all they are worth, they are not going to rise to a surface-fished imitative pattern no matter how skilfully presented. However, try a Whisky or a Nailer Fly or a Leprechaun on a high density line and fish it at their level – then watch for their response.

Of course, we often read of "mindless lure stripping". Take a walk round any fishery, and you will find unthinking anglers doing just that. Look again, and you will also discover anglers "mindlessly" pulling nymphs and flies through the water.

The subtleties and arts of fishing the nymph and dry fly on stillwater may not, then, be practised by all, but they are readily recognised by most of us. An increasing number of thoughtful anglers is aware that the practice of lure fishing is also a mystique to be acquired.

It offers a variety of tactics to be employed on an intelligent appraisal of season and time of day, of weather and water conditions. The thinking lure fisherman has at his disposal a range of flies with differing characteristics. Looking at wings alone, they may be streamers (feathers), bucktail (hair), marabou or rabbit, each with its own action in the water. He may be fishing a big marabou lure like an Appetiser deeply on a lead impregnated line, or another marabou lure like a Poodle as a nymph on a floating line. An orange fly like a Whisky may be retrieved quickly in high summer for aggressive rainbows whilst in early season a black fly, say a Black Chenille, is pulled back slowly and deeply. He will have his days for his wake flies like the Muddler; the rise and fall of his Nobblers; the slow downward flutter of his Missionary, the dependability of a Sweeny Todd or a Baby Doll; the fry-imitating qualities of his Jack

Frost or Sinfoil's Fry or Mylar Minnow; the patience-demanding inert floaters like Wadham's Floating Fry. And he may be searching through a volume of water, often for an invisible prize, experimenting with depth and speed and variation of retrieve until a fish responds. Even then that response may be a slow suck, a vicious take, a gentle tap or a sudden heaviness. Yes, it is a mystique all right.

What we want to do in this book is to introduce you to the array of patterns that you can have at your disposal, each supreme in its own way, with its own particular applications and uses, and then show you how to tie them. The instructions are detailed so that the beginner will quickly develop the confidence to tie good, durable and attractive lures, whilst for the more experienced dresser there is a wealth of incidental expertise which he will readily appreciate and add, if necessary, to his own skills. In following the instructions, the reader will acquire good, methodical tying habits which will enable him to produce flies which are pleasing to look at, pleasing to use, and, best of all, pleasing to the trout.

We have attempted to write the book in a personal way, so that our readers are aware that our fishing experiences have much in common with theirs. We write thus in the first person, and so "I" in the introductions to the lures refers to Kenneth Robson, and in the tying instructions and dressings to Bob Carnill.

BEEKAY PUBLISHERS
WITHY POOL
BEDFORD ROAD
HENLOW CAMP,
BEDS. SG16 6EA
ENGLAND

ISBN 0 947674 11 X

Typeset by Butler & Tanner Ltd., Frome and London
Printed by Castle Cary Press, Somerset

Dressed to Kill

Seventy Successful Trout Lures

FLY DRESSING AND PHOTOGRAPHY BY
BOB CARNILL
AND
RESEARCH AND COLLATION BY
KENNETH ROBSON

BEEKAY PUBLISHERS

Ace of Spades

This certainly is a black ace for you to play as an opening gambit at the beginning of the season. David Collyer, who invented the fly in 1973, wished to devise a lure as successful as the Black Lure but avoiding its chief weakness, namely the feather wing twisting round under the hook points, thus destroying its proper swimming posture. He looked for something with a more solid silhouette than the hair wing of say a Sweeny Todd, and settled on a black hen hackle wing tied in the matuka style which originated in New Zealand.

This particular feature consists of the two or four feathers used for the wings having their fibres stripped from one side of the hackle for the length of the hook shank, and the upright fibres bound to the shank by the ribbing. The tips of the hackles are left intact to protrude past the hook bend to form the tail. David then gave the fly a roof wing of dark bronze mallard feather.

He first tried out the Ace of Spades at Weir Wood reservoir, now happily reopened as a trout fishery, by the way. The lure proved highly successful, and he told me recently that he still considers it by far and away his best fly. He feels that it is especially good at taking

1

the rather larger fish. He has also found it effective at Chew Valley in murky conditions when its dense silhouette adds to its visibility. It can be fished at varying levels in the water on a slow sinker or floater and at different retrieval speeds. In late April this year, I watched an angler take four fish in a short time during a hatch of black buzzers in late evening at Hanningfield whilst I took one. He was using a small Ace of Spades on the point, and on the dropper he had a size 12 standard hook with a short black marabou tail with the spare marabou wrapped round the body and oval silver tinsel ribbed. This combination he fished very very slowly, and that particular evening had two fish on the Ace of Spades and two on the dropper fly. He told me that the conventional buzzer imitations that I was using frequently did not work. The next week, the small Ace of Spades and its black cousin on the dropper fished ultra slowly on a floater brought success for me also.

How to tie

Hook:	L/S 6–12
Silk:	Black
Rib:	Oval silver tinsel
Body:	Black chenille
Wing:	Two dyed black hen hackles tied matuka style as a crest. Four may be used to create a denser image.
Overwing:	Dark bronze mallard
Hackle:	Guinea fowl tied as a false beard.

Run waxed silk from immediately behind the eye of the hook down the shank in neat, butting turns, and stop opposite the point of the hook. At this position, catch in a short length of oval silver tinsel, then continue with the silk to a point just before the bend begins, lashing down the tinsel as you go. With your very first turn of the tying silk returning up the shank, catch in a length of medium gauge black chenille by its stripped central core, and then continue up the shank, again in neat, butting turns, lashing down the butt of the stripped core as you go. Stop the silk a short distance from the eye of the hook, allowing just enough space for the hackle and the head of the lure.

   The chenille can now be wound along the shank in neat, touching turns and, on reaching the anchored silk, tied off with three firm turns of the silk. Next, cut away the waste chenille, and cover the raw butt end with turns of the tying silk. The silk is now returned to the head end of the body ready to receive the wing.

For the wing, select two or four large, matching hen hackles, and align them tip on tip, and back to back. Grip the feathers tightly in this position while the base flue and fibres are stripped away to leave the overall length of the hackles exactly right for the finished wing. Having done this, the underside fibres of the wing are then stripped away for a distance equivalent to the length of the chenille body, leaving fibres on both sides of the central stem at the tip which will form the tail of the lure. Now offer the wing up for tying in by positioning it over the back of the body so that the bottom-most fibres of the tail come level with the rear end of the chenille body. Whilst in this position, secure the wings in place by taking four or five turns of the tying silk over the stripped hackle stems at the head end of the lure. This done, let the silk hang at anchor. The tinsel can now be wound back up the body in equal, open spirals, passing it carefully through the crest of hen hackle fibres as you go. On reaching the silk, lash the tinsel down firmly, and cut away the waste end and also the waste hackle stems.

The hook is now reversed in the vice ready to receive the beard hackle of speckled guinea fowl fibres. After tying in the fibres, trim away the waste ends, cover their butt ends with turns of the tying silk, and then return the silk close up to the commencement of the wing ready to receive the overwing. The hook is now returned to its original position.

The final stage, that of tying in the bronze mallard overwing, is the most difficult part in the whole dressing of the Ace of Spades. To accomplish this in the easiest possible manner, it is important to use two slips of the best quality bronze mallard you can afford or find. The slips should be equivalent in width to two wings, and should be as square as possible at their tips.

Having cut two slips of equal width, lay them one on top of the other, tip on tip (concave on convex), and then fold them equally over the crest of matuka'd hackles. Hold in this position, pinched between the finger and thumb of the left hand, and secure in the normal way using several pinch and loops. Successfully accomplished, the waste ends can then be cut away, a neat head formed with the tying silk and whip finished. Two coats of cellire varnish will complete the lure.

The Alexandra Demon

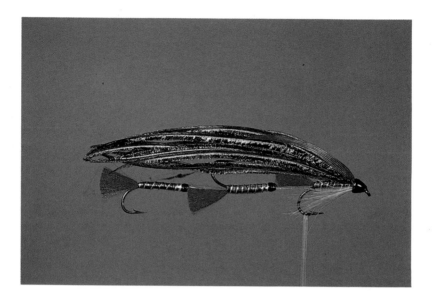

Most people tend to associate lure fishing with the boom in stillwater trouting in the 1950s and 1960s. The Alexandra salmon fly was used on Blagdon as early as the First World War, and the Alexandra Demon was one of the "Dr Evelyn" lures introduced by Hardy Brothers as early as 1935. Primarily designed as a deadly lure for sea trout, it was used with equal success for brown trout on lochs and reservoirs. Bob recollects that when he took up trout fishing in the early 1960s three hook lures or Terrors and Demons were very much in vogue amongst stillwater trout fishermen. However, after the mid-sixties they slipped from favour, giving way to tandem or extra large single hook lures. As they were very efficient trout catchers, the only apparent reason they lost their appeal may have been the modern trout fisherman's reluctance to construct the labour intensive mounts.

However, as with most fashions, things usually come full circle, and since the advent of lead-lining the three hook lure seems to be making a comeback. Nottingham's top tackle dealer and fly fishing expert Tom Saville says "In recent years, the keen reservoir trout fisher, especially if he uses deeply sunk lines when boat fishing, has recognised the effectiveness of the 'Demon' or three hook lure, made up with either long shanked or normal shanked hooks. This type of assembly gives a lure an overall length of up to 10 cms imitating a sizable baitfish, yet makes for ease of hooking. Using a single hook of such size, it would be virtually impossible to hook fish securely with the comparatively limited power of a trout fly rod."

In his early days on the reservoirs, Bob used to cast three hook lures as a matter of course on standard trout gear. His favourites were the Black Terror (similar dressing to the Black Lure) for deep, early season fishing, the Blue and Silver Terror in bright, cold conditions, particularly if the water was clear, and the Alexandra Demon should he want something in between. Learning the skill of constructing your own mounts is well worthwhile, so why not do so and add the Alexandra Demon to your repertoire of lures.

How to tie

Hooks:	Three size 8 or 10 standard shanks, tied in tandem with the middle hook facing upwards
Monofilament mount:	A double strand of stiff twelve pound Tynex is ideal
Silk:	Black
Tails:	Scarlet or crimson floss or fine wool. DF materials such as Datam glo-brite numbers three and four, and DRF fire-orange nylon are very useful
Body:	Flat silver tinsel
Rib:	Fine silver wire
Wing:	A generous bunch of fine peacock herl fibres with a slip of scarlet fibres (ibis substitute) on either side

To give this lure a neater, more streamlined effect, it is best to remove the eyes from the rear and middle hooks. The way I do it is to bury the hook deep into the vice with just the eye left protruding. It is then gripped in a pair of pliers or forceps and cracked smartly backwards.

Place the prepared hook in the vice in the normal way, and then run waxed silk from a point just before the bend begins, up the shank in neat, butting turns and stop a short distance (approximately 1 mm) from the end. Now take two 7 cm lengths of stiff nylon monofilament and cut a tapered end to each piece. This done, line the tapers up and lash them on top of the shank, side by side, with three or four turns of the silk travelling back down the shank. The tapered ends should be positioned immediately above the point of the hook. Now take a tube of Superglue and apply a little along the length of the two strands of monofilament including the three or four lashings of silk. The amount of glue used should be just enough to run between the strands and onto the shank. After applying the glue, quickly continue lashing the monofilament to the top of the shank with firm, butting turns until the end of the monofilament is reached. At this point, catch in a short length of fine silver wire, and then continue with the silk to a point just before the bend begins. The silk can now be left to hang at anchor.

Having prepared the tail material, offer it up and tie in on top of the shank so that the forward-facing cropped ends come level with the tapered ends of the lashed down monofilament. This will help to maintain a level base on which to lay the silver tinsel body. Continue with the silk up the shank in neat, butting turns, lashing down the tail material as you go, and stop a short distance from the end.

The flat silver tinsel, or lurex if you prefer it, can now be tied in and wound down the shank to the tail and back again. On reaching the anchored silk, tie off the tinsel and cut away the waste. Winding flat silver tinsel in neat, touching turns down and back again over itself, gives the best possible finish to a tinsel body. The body can now be ribbed with tight, equally spaced turns of the silver wire. On reaching the silk, tie off, cut away the waste, form a neat head with the silk and whip finish. Before removing the hook from the vice, grasp the tail, pull taut and crop to length. This hook can now be removed from the vice and replaced by another eyeless hook.

As before, the silk is introduced to the shank of the hook at a point just before the bend begins, and then run in touching turns up the shank to within a very short distance of the end. The first hook with the monofilament strand attached is now offered up for tying in. To do this, first turn the hook over so that it is presented at 90 degrees to the one now held in the vice, then lower the two strands onto the top of the hook and secure in exactly the same way as was the first. The distance between the two hooks should be approximately 5 mm from the bend of the second hook to the end (the point where the eye has been removed) of the rear hook. The rest of the body can now be completed using the same method as for the previous body.

The third or leading hook can now be placed in the vice and the two strands of monofilament secured in the usual way. However, before completing the initial lashing down process, lift the two strands slightly and crop them away at a low, shallow angle to the shank at a position approximately two thirds the way back to the eye. This done, cover the tapered ends with firm turns of the silk. The body and tail can now be added as before, then, on completion, turn the hook over in the vice and add a beard hackle of bright blue cock hackle fibres. After cropping away the waste ends of the hackle fibres and covering their butts with firm turns of silk, a small whip finish or a couple of half hitches is performed to secure the silk; because it is at this point that the heads of the two rear hooks should be varnished. If this is left until the lure is completed, then there is a real risk of the wing also becoming adhered. Once the varnish has gone-off, the hook is returned to the vice ready to receive the wing. For the wing, select about fourteen fine peacock herls of the kind found lower down the tail feather, place them end on end, and then tie in on top of the shank. The length of the wing should be gauged to come level with the tail of the rear hook. After lashing the herls into place, crop away the waste ends and cover their butts with firm turns of silk.

The two slips of red ibis substitute can now be added to either side of the wing, after which a neat head is formed with the tying silk and whip finished. Two coats of cellire varnish will complete the lure.

Appetiser

Introduced by Bob Church in 1973, this was one of the first marabou lures. Most of the marabou now used is a substitute from the legs of turkeys. Appetiser was designed to tempt the larger trout when they were feeding on fry during the latter part of the season on the big reservoirs. One of Bob Church's specialised techniques fishing deep water hot spots from a boat was to use a lead-impregnated line, an 18 feet untapered leader of 8 lb breaking strain and a size 6 long shank Appetiser or even a big, special extra long shanked hook up to 9 cm in length. Fished in this manner, the lure has taken more specimen fish for him than any other except the White Marabou Muddler.

Bob Carnill also has a special use for a large tandem Appetiser dressed on size 6 or even size 4 longshanks to tackle trout browsing on sub-surface snails in the weeded shallows of Rutland Water from middle to late summer. The lure is presented on a long leader and floating line from a drifting boat into an area of shallow, well-weeded water and retrieved quite quickly with long pulls on the line to throw up a sub-surface wake. A secondary wake or a sudden explosive slash at the lure, and you are in business. Needless to say, an angle between the rod and the line is essential at all times during the retrieve.

Of course, the Appetiser does not imitate a snail, but Bob suggests that a large lure suddenly appearing in, and dashing through, a trout's feeding territory will often produce a reflex response from a preocupied snail-feeder. His proof? After catching trout on numerous occasions using this technique he examined their stomach contents. Each time they were crammed solid with snail.

The Appetiser should be stocked in a wide range of sizes. We have both had a great deal of success in the smaller 8 and 10 sizes. Bob's theory is that when trout seem attracted to, and yet tend to shy away from an all-white lure, as quite often happens in bright light and gin clear water, the Appetiser comes into its own.

How to tie

Hook:	L/S 6–8
Silk:	Black
Tail:	Mixed orange and dark green cock hackle fibres, and just a few fibres of silver mallard
Rib:	Flat silver tinsel
Body:	White chenille, preferably daylight fluorescent
Wing:	White marabou, large spray
Overwing:	Natural grey squirrel tail
Throat hackle:	As for tail

Run waxed silk from immediately behind the eye of the hook, down the shank in neat, butting turns, and stop opposite the point. Now take a bunch of mixed orange and dark green cock hackle fibres into which a few silver mallard fibres have been intermingled, and tie in on top of the shank to form the tail of the lure. Having done this, continue with the silk down the shank, lashing the tail firmly into place on top of the shank as you go, and stop at a point just before the bend begins.

With your very first turn of the silk returning up the shank, catch in a length of medium width flat silver tinsel, and with your second turn, catch in a length of white chenille by its stripped central core. The silk can now be returned back up the shank in neat, butting turns, lashing down the butt ends of the tinsel and chenille core as you go. Stop the silk a short distance from the eye leaving just enough space for the wing and the throat hackle.

9

The chenille can now be wound up the shank in neat, butting turns and, on reaching the anchored silk, tied down with three firm turns of the silk. The waste chenille is then cut away. Now take hold of the tinsel and wind over the body in firm, equally spaced turns. On reaching the anchored silk, tie down and cut away the waste tinsel. The raw ends of both tinsel and chenille core can now be covered with firm turns of the silk which is then returned to the head end of the body. The hook is now turned over in the vice ready to receive the beard hackle.

Prepare the hackle fibres in exactly the same way as used for the tail, but be a little more generous with the overall amount. After tying the hackle fibres in, cut away their waste ends and cover the butts with firm turns of silk. The hook is now returned to its original position in the vice.

A large spray of white marabou can now be tied in to lie over the back of the lure. The length of this wing should extend slightly beyond the tip of the tail. After tying the marabou in, crop away the waste ends at as shallow an angle to the shank as possible, and then cover the butt ends with firm turns of the tying silk. It cannot be emphasised enough how important it is that the marabou be tied in as tightly as possible so as to create a firm base on which to tie the overwing of non-compressible grey squirrel tail hairs.

Select a small bunch of hair from a grey squirrel tail, taking care to keep the tips in line, and tie in to lie over the top of the marabou wing. Make the turns of silk as tight as the strength of the silk will allow, and it is not a bad idea to bed the hair down into a drop of cellire varnish. Once the overwing is tied firmly into place, crop away the waste ends and cover their butts with further firm turns of the tying silk. All that remains is to form a neat head with the silk, whip finish and varnish.

Baby Doll

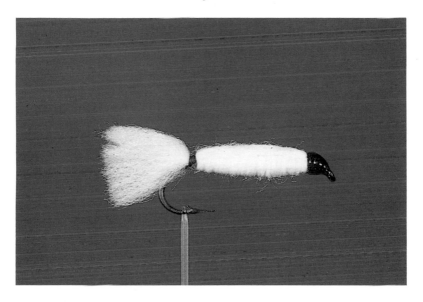

A lure created by Brian Kench in 1971 and publicised by Bob Church which has had consistent and astonishing success. The fly has "no moving parts", and its deadliness is almost certainly due to the high visibility of its brilliant white nylon wool or daylight fluorescent white wool. This is why Bob suggests in his dressing that fingers be scrubbed scrupulously clean before tying. Bob Church replaces his patterns after just one day's use.

The Baby Doll has been known to take fish on virtually every type of stillwater under all conditions and depths, and any part of the season or day. However, early in the season when fish are not in their full vigour and disinclined to chase anything moving too quickly, it works best being allowed to sink to or near the bottom and given a slow retrieve. Be on the alert for your Baby Doll being taken on the drop. Again, in those last desperate minutes before closing time when trout are sometimes rising to tiny and inscrutable flies, a Baby Doll ripped through the surface may produce a ferocious grab to complete your limit.

Baby Dolls can be tied in a variety of colours such as orange, scarlet and yellow. Lime green is particularly profitable, and recently a peach colour has proved very killing.

Two other variations that Bob has fished most frequently, and consequently most successfully, are the Peppermint Doll and the DF Pink Doll.

The Peppermint Doll is merely the original with the addition of two lengths of DRF signal-green fuzz wool tied in and laid along the side. In other words, in the same position as one expects to see the lateral line. He finds it very useful indeed during low light conditions, that is early morning and late evening, or when there is a touch of colour in the water, or when fishing deep.

The DF Pink Doll, by contrast, comes into its own during warm-water conditions from July to September fished on a floating line quite close to the surface. Sometimes great sport can be enjoyed when using this pattern on the point in conjunction with a longshank size 8 Red Palmer on a dropper positioned three to four feet above. This combination is particularly useful when fishing in and around weed beds.

How to tie

Hook:	L/S 6–10
Silk:	Black
Body:	Brilliant white nylon wool or daylight fluorescent white wool. Sirdar brand suggested
Tail & back:	As body. A 12 mm tail with the wool shredded to produce a bushy and fish-like tail

Before attempting to tie the Baby Doll, it is absolutely essential that the fingers are scrubbed scrupulously clean, otherwise the brilliance and the daylight fluorescent properties of the wool will be lost.

Run waxed silk from immediately behind the eye of the hook down the shank in neat, butting turns, and stop at a point just before the hook bend begins. Now take three strands of white DF wool, the length of which should be sufficient to overhang both the finished tail position and the eye of the hook, lay them together as one, and then tie them in on top of the hook shank at this point. Now lift the forward-facing strands of wool, lay them back over the tail, and then return the tying silk back up the shank in neat, butting turns to a position a short distance from the eye.

A single length of white DF wool is now tied in at this point, wound down the shank to the tail, and then back again to the anchored silk. On reaching the silk, tie off with three or four turns of the silk, cut away the waste wool at as shallow an angle to the shank as possible, and then cover the raw butt ends of the wool with firm turns of the silk. The fish-like shape of the body is achieved by varying the closeness of the laps of wool, and also by unspinning the ply of the wool on reaching the tail and head ends so as to make it lie much flatter.

The three strands of wool which form the back of the lure are now laid into position, drawn tightly, and secured with three or four firm turns of the tying silk. The waste wool is now cut away, again at a shallow angle, and a neat head formed with the tying silk before completing with the usual whip finish. All that remains to complete the Baby Doll is to crop the tail to length, flare out the individual fibres, and varnish the head.

Badger Lure

This is a pattern which ranks alongside the Black Lure as one of the early and popular lures devised to meet the special conditions of the bigger reservoirs. It is particularly good for those hot, late summer days when bays are teeming with sticklebacks or perch fry, and brown trout and rainbows come sweeping in and mopping up the little fish as they go. The Badger Lure is then best fished with a floating line and long leader of at least 5 lb breaking strain. Try to cast a metre or so in front of the cruising fish and draw your lure across his path. If nothing happens, leave your fly in the water and give it a brief slow pull at intervals. Trout often return to pick off at leisure those fry they have wounded in their first charge. Takes can often be savage in these circumstances. A beautifully conditioned 3 lb brownie I took recently at Chew Valley Lake had the lure at the very back of its throat.

Some anglers find the tandem lure cumbersome, and prefer a single hook with the matuka style of winging which avoids the wing feather tangling in the bend of the hook and around the barb. Bob explains how to tie matuka style in the dressing of the Red and Black Matuka.

14

A Badger Matuka can be used earlier in the season from boat or bank with a slow-sinker shooting head or a fast sinker. If you experience a number of taps which do not develop into takes, the trout may be shy of your big lure, and the answer then is to drop down a size or two.

How to tie

Hooks:	Two L/S 10's in tandem
Silk:	Orange
Bodies:	Fluorescent orange wool
Ribs:	Fine oval silver tinsel
Throat:	Hot-orange cock hackle fibres
Wings:	Two or four large badger cock hackles back to back and as long as the hooks
Eyes:	Two jungle cock (or substitute) feathers tied in short

There are several ways in which tandem and treble hook lure rigs can be assembled, but nowadays my favourite method is to use two lengths of stiff nylon monofilament laid side by side, with the eye(s) of the rear hook(s) removed in order to give the overall appearance of the lure a much more streamlined effect. The assembly of the Badger Lure mount is identical to that described for the Alexandra Demon on page 5, the only difference being that two hooks are used as opposed to three, and both hooks are presented with the bends facing downwards.

So, having fixed the two strands of monofilament to what will be the rear hook, and with the silk hanging at anchor at a position opposite the point of the hook, a length of number 14 oval silver tinsel can now be caught in, and the silk then taken down the shank in neat, butting turns, lashing down the tinsel as you go, to stop at a point just before the bend begins.

With your very first turn of the silk returning up the shank, catch in a length of DF wool, and then continue along the shank in neat, butting turns to within a short distance at the end, and there let the silk hang at anchor. The orange wool can now be wound up the shank in neat, butting turns and, on reaching the anchored silk, tied off with three firm turns of the silk and the waste wool cut away. This is then followed by the oval silver tinsel which is wound over the wool body in firm, equally spaced open spirals. On reaching the anchored silk the tinsel is tied off, the waste cut away, and then a neat head formed with the silk and whip finished. The front hook can now be attached to the two monofilament strands in exactly the same way as described for the Alexandra Demon, and then the body formed the same way as was the rear hook of this mount.

The rig is now turned over in the vice ready to receive the beard or false hackle. Now select a large cock hackle dyed hot-orange and strip away from it a fairly generous bunch of fibres, taking care to keep their tips in line. This done, offer the bunch of fibres up and tie in to form a nice spray around the uppermost part of the shank. Now cut away the waste ends of the hackle fibres and cover their butts with firm turns of silk. The hook can now be returned to its original position in the vice and the silk wound up to the head end of the body ready to receive the wing.

For the wing, select two or four large, matching badger hackles and align them tip on tip, and back to back. Grip the feathers tightly in this position while all the base flue and sufficient fibres are stripped away to leave the overall length of the hackles exactly right for the finished wing. The wing can now be offered up and tied in by lashing the stripped stems with four or five very firm turns of the silk travelling in the direction of the hook eye. The excess stems can now be cropped away at a shallow angle to the shank and their butts covered with very firm turns of the silk which is then returned back down the shank to the commencement of the wing.

Two jungle cock feathers (or substitute) are now positioned one on either side of the wing, and secured there with touching turns of the silk travelling towards the eye of the hook. Just before the eye is reached, complete the head with the usual whip finish and cut away the silk. Two coats of cellire varnish to the head will complete the lure.

Banded Squirrel Bucktail

This is a bucktail lure devised by Taff Price which has been successful for him on a number of reservoirs including Hanningfield. I also have found it a very useful fish taker at Hanningfield. It can be fished, like most lures, with a variable retrieve, and at differing depths according to conditions and the time of the year. I have done best with it early in the season fished deeply and slowly on a shooting head aquasink line. However, it will also work later on using a floating line and a steady retrieve. The squirrel hair when wet gives the fly a long, slim profile which aids sinking.

How to tie

Hook:	L/S 6–10
Silk:	Black
Tail:	Red and white cock hackle fibres
Rib:	Fine oval silver tinsel
Body:	Mauve wool
Wing:	Grey squirrel tail
Hackle:	False hackle of red and white cock hackle fibres

Run waxed silk from immediately behind the eye of the hook, down the shank in neat, butting turns and stop at a point opposite the hook point. Now take a dyed red and a natural white cock hackle, and strip away equal amounts of fibres from each feather, taking care to keep their tips in line. The fibres are then mixed together by gently rolling them between finger and thumb. The fibres are then offered up and tied in on top of the shank to form the tail of the lure. The silk can now be continued down the shank in neat, butting turns, tying down the tail as you go, and stopped at a position just before the bend begins.

With your very first turn of the tying silk returning up the shank, catch in a length of fine oval silver, and with your second turn a length of mauve wool. The silk is then returned up the shank in neat, butting turns, lashing down the butt ends of tinsel and wool as you go, to stop a short distance from the eye allowing just enough room for the beard hackle and the wing. The wool can now be wound up the shank in neat, butting turns and, on reaching the anchored silk, tie down with three firm turns of the silk. The waste wool is then cut away. Now take hold of the tinsel and rib the wool body with firm, open spirals. On reaching the silk, tie the tinsel down and cut away the waste. The raw ends of the wool and tinsel can now be covered with firm turns of the silk which is then returned to the head end of the body ready to receive the hackle.

First, turn the hook over in the vice, and then prepare the hackle in exactly the same way as was used for the tail, but be a little more generous with the overall amount. Having prepared the fibres for the beard hackle, offer them up and tie in to form a nice spray around the uppermost portion of the shank. This done, cut away the waste ends of the fibres and cover their butts with firm turns of the silk. The hook can now be returned to its original position in the vice, and the silk to the head end of the body to receive the wing.

To form the wing, select a bunch of hair as it lies in its natural position on the tail and gently pull it upright. Provided that the grip is not too tight, the tips of the individual hairs will gradually come into line as they are drawn upwards. As soon as this occurs, tighten the grip on the hair and crop it away at the roots. The next job is to comb out any underfur and short or broken hairs.

Now, gripping the bunch of hair between the finger and thumb of the right hand by its cut ends, lower it down onto the top of the shank to measure for length. This measured grip is then taken up by the finger and thumb of the left hand. The bunch is then lifted clear of the shank while a drop of fine cellire varnish is applied to the bed of tying silk on top of the hook shank onto which the hair is to be tied. The bunch can now be lowered back into its measured place and secured with four or five very firm turns of the silk travelling in the direction of the hook eye. The finger and thumb grip can now be removed to check that all has gone well. If satisfied, re-establish the grip on the wing whilst the waste hair is cropped away at as shallow an angle as is possible. This done, another drop of cellire is applied to the cropped ends of the hair. This will disappear as capillary action draws the fine varnish into the cut ends. The hair wing is now held in place while the tying silk is taken forward in very firm touching turns. Any excess varnish will now be squeezed out of the cut ends by the pressure of the silk, and should be wiped away and not allowed to foul the eye.

After the initial tying down of the wing, the silk is then returned up the head still using very tight turns, until it comes to within a very short distance of the first turns of silk that originally secured the bunch of hair. Several more turns of silk are now applied but with only a light pressure. These turns should cover the original two or three turns, and then two or three more are allowed to run onto the start of the wing, still under light presssure. This manoeuvre will have the effect of giving the wing a nice low lie or angle to the body. The silk can now be returned towards the eye, forming a nice neat head as you go. Just before the eye is reached, finish the head off with the usual whip finish. Two coats of cellire to the head will complete the lure.

Beastie Lure (Voodoo)

Although Geoffrey Bucknall has recently modified his Beastie Lure and renamed it the Voodoo, Bob and I have decided to leave the entry under its original name as it holds a special place in the development of the leadhead type of lure. Geoff was inspired to add two layers of fine lead wire to the head of this lure after watching his friend, Dr Tony Richards, clip on a swan shot to the head of a normal marabou lure whilst fishing at Hanningfield. The Beastie also involved the deployment of a marabou wing twice the length of the hook shank so that this was made to vibrate enticingly by the weighted head as the fly dipped and rose according to the way it was retrieved.

In his book, *Modern Techniques of Still Water Fishing*, Geoff places a good deal of emphasis on the killing properties of the lure's diving action. Though the lure may look extremely bulky when dry, it slims down considerably once it is wet.

For the Voodoo, Geoff replaces the body of black floss silk with fluorescent lime floss. The false hackle and underwing are now fluorescent lime-green marabou, and the orange theme used there has been transferred to the wing which is now a rich hot-orange marabou. He regards this as a perch fry imitation. He also has a version which uses fluorescent green as hackle and underwing, but retains black marabou for the main wing as in the original Beastie.

How to tie

Hook:	L/S streamer 6
Silk:	Black
Rib:	Flat silver tinsel
Body:	Black floss silk
False hackle:	Small bouquet of orange marabou
Underwing:	Longer strip of orange marabou feather
Wing:	Two black marabou plumes tied in back to back so that they extend well 'beyond the hook bend, about as long again as the hook shank
Cheek:	Black and white barred silver pheasant flank feathers tied in on either side of the hook, the central stalks level with the shank. Jungle cock or substitute overlaid onto the cheek
Head:	Two layers of lead wire covering about 6 mms of shank

Run waxed silk from immediately behind the eye of the hook down the shank in neat, butting turns, and stop just before the bend begins. With your very first turn of the tying silk returning up the shank, catch in a length of flat silver tinsel, and then continue up the shank in neat, butting turns, lashing down the raw end of the tinsel as you go. Stop the silk 6 mms from the eye. At this point, a length of black floss silk is tied in, and then wound down the shank in neat, touching turns until the end of the foundation laps of tying silk are reached. The floss is then returned back up the shank in a similar manner to the anchored silk. On reaching the tying silk, the floss can then be tied off with three firm turns of the silk and the waste floss cut away. Now take hold of the tinsel, and rib the floss body with firm, equally spaced, open spirals. On reaching the anchored silk, tie the tinsel down with three firm turns and then cut away the waste. The raw ends of the tinsel and floss silk can now be covered with firm laps of the tying silk which is then returned to the head end of the body.

We are now ready for the false hackle, so reverse the hook in the vice in the usual way. For the false hackle, we will require just a small bouquet of orange marabou fibres which will extend to the bend of the hook. After tying the marabou hackle in and cutting

21

away the waste butts, the hook can then be returned to its original position in the vice. The underwing which consists of another slightly more generous bunch of orange marabou, is now tied in on top of the hook shank to extend well beyond the bend of the hook. After cropping away the waste ends of the underwing, the butts of both hackle and underwing can be covered with firm turns of the tying silk which is then returned to the commencement of the wing. It is important when tying down any materials in the 6 mm space left between the body and the eye of the hook to keep the bed of tying silk as level and as firm as possible, because this will eventually form the bed on which the two layers of lead wire is wound.

Now select two whole black marabou plumes, and tie them in back to back, one on either side of the shank, so that they extend at least one full hook's length behind the bend of the hook. This done, crop away their waste ends, and cover with firm turns of the tying silk. Now return the silk to the start of the wing ready to receive the cheeks. For the cheeks, select two matching silver pheasant flank feathers, and strip away all the base flue to reveal a section of central stalk. Place the prepared feathers one on either side of the black marabou wing with their stalks level with the shank, and secure with several firm turns of the silk. Now take two jungle cock, or substitute, feathers and overlay them, one on either side, onto the silver pheasant cheeks. Position the jungle cocks so that they lie centrally with their stalks level with the hook shank. Secure them in this position with several turns of the tying silk, then cut away the waste ends of the jungle cock and the stalks of the silver pheasant flank feathers, and cover their butts with firm turns of the silk travelling towards the eye.

With the silk now hanging at anchor just behind the eye, the lead head can be applied. Take a length of lead wire, and tie it in close to the eye. The wire is now wound in touching turns along the 6 mm space which has been allotted to it until the wing and the false hackle are reached, and then back again to the waiting silk where it is tied down and the waste cut away. The raw end of the lead wire can now be covered with the tying silk, a small neat head formed and then whip finished. The head is now given a good soaking with superglue to fix the lead permanently in place, and then put to one side to dry out completely. Once the head is dry, a couple of coats of polyurethane varnish will complete the lure.

Black and Orange Marabou

John Veniard gave a dressing for a marabou winged fly as early as 1970 in his *Reservoir and Lake Flies*, and two years later Taff Price gave us the Black and Orange Marabou as a variation of the Black Marabou. Here again is an example of orange adding something to a fly, and this one has proved successful for Taff Price time and time again.

Apart from the usual ways of retrieving marabou type flies, John Wadham offers an interesting variation by fishing them in a similar manner to nymphs, finding marabou the ideal medium for this technique. Fished on a lee shore with a nymph on a dropper near the lure, with wind from right to left, he allows it to come round on a floating line and watches it near the rod tip for any movement, and strikes at the merest sign. Another method down wind is to retrieve with a fast figure of eight or with a long, slow pull with a long pause after it, watching the line for a slight draw. This method allows the lure to come to the water surface and then flutter enticingly down again. Black gives him the best results, but he also includes orange as a choice, so the Black and Orange Marabou should meet the bill.

Incidentally, John recommends the best times as dull days, early mornings and evenings.

How to tie

Hook:	D/E L/S 8
Silk:	Black
Tail:	Orange cock hackle fibres
Rib:	Oval gold tinsel
Body:	Flat gold tinsel or lurex
Wing:	Bunch of black marabou
Cheeks:	Jungle cock or substitute, optional
Hackle:	Bunch of orange cock hackle fibres

Run waxed silk from immediately behind the eye of the hook down the shank in neat, butting turns, and stop opposite the point of the hook. Now take a large, orange-dyed cock hackle and strip away from it a small bunch of fibres, taking care to keep their tips in line. The bunch of fibres is then offered up, and tied in on top of the shank. Whilst holding the tail fibres in position, continue with the silk in neat, butting turns to a point just before the bend begins.

With your very first turn of the silk returning up the shank, catch in the oval gold tinsel, and then continue up the shank in neat, butting turns, tying down the butt end of the oval tinsel as you go. Stop the silk a short distance from the eye of the hook, allowing just enough space for the wing and hackle. Now catch in at this point a length of medium width flat gold tinsel, or lurex if you prefer it, with three firm turns of the silk. The tinsel can then be wound down the shank in neat, touching turns until the last lap of the foundation silk is reached. On reaching this point, the tinsel is then returned back up the shank, again in touching turns, and on reaching the anchored silk, tied down and the waste cut away. This is then followed by the oval gold tinsel which is wound over the gold tinsel body or lurex in firm, open and equally spaced spirals until the anchored silk is reached. On reaching the silk, tie the oval tinsel down and snip away the waste. The raw ends of both the flat and oval tinsel can now be covered with neat turns of the tying silk travelling in the direction of the eye. This done, the silk is returned to the head end of the body ready to receive the beard or false hackle.

First, turn the hook over in the vice. Now select another large, orange-dyed cock hackle and strip away from it a fairly generous bunch of fibres, taking care once again to keep the tips in line. Having prepared the fibres for the beard hackle, offer them up, and tie in to form a nice spray around the uppermost portion of the shank. This done, cut away the waste ends of the fibres, and cover their butts with firm turns of the silk. The hook can now be returned to its original position in the vice, and the silk to the head end of the body ready to receive the wing.

The wing for the Black and Orange Marabou is, as its name suggests, a fairly generous bunch or spray of black marabou fibres, and it is prepared by spinning them into a shuttlecock formation as described for the head and tail plumes of the Cat's Whisker on page 50. So, having prepared the plume of marabou, it can now be tied in on top of the hook shank immediately above the commencement of the beard hackle. The length of wing to aim for is one that extends just slightly beyond the tip of the tail fibres.

Having tied the wing in, and cropped away the waste butt ends at a shallow angle to the shank, the butts can then be covered with firm turns of the silk which is then returned to the commencement of the wing ready to receive the cheeks. Select two matching jungle cock eye feathers, and strip away the unwanted flue and superfluous fibre from below the eye. Now position one of the prepared feathers on either side of the marabou wing, and secure in place with several turns of the tying silk travelling in the direction of the eye of the hook. Once the eye feathers are securely and satisfactorily positioned, their waste ends can be snipped away, and a neat head formed with the tying silk. Finish the head off with the usual whip finish and two coats of cellire varnish.

Black Bear's Hair Lure

This is a variation on the black lure theme which you can add to your Black Chenilles and Vivas. It was devised originally by Cliff Henry and recommended by John Goddard. John tells me that when he fishes a lure, which is not very often, he still has great faith in this particular lure. He emphasises, however, that it must be dressed correctly, and that the black bear hair on the narrow strip of skin must overhang the bend so that it gives an undulating motion to the lure when retrieved.

He advises that it be fished on either a floating or sinking line with variable retrieves, but with pauses to activate the bear's hair. It will take trout early on fished near the bottom, and, later in summer, can be tried just below the surface.

How to tie

Hook: D/E L/S 8–10
Silk: Black
Rib: Oval silver tinsel

Body: Black seal's fur
Wing: Thin strip of black bear's skin approximately 3 mms wide
          with long hair attached cut 6 to 8 mms longer than the hook
          shank. Dyed-black rabbit's fur is a suitable substitute

Run waxed silk from immediately behind the eye of the hook down the shank in neat, butting turns, and stop opposite the point of the hook. Now catch in 8 to 10 cms of oval silver tinsel by its tip, and then continue with the silk down the shank, lashing down the tinsel as you go. Stop the silk just before the bend begins, leaving the tinsel trailing beyond the bend.

The silk is now dubbed with black seal's fur, and a fairly thick body formed as the silk is wound back up the shank towards the eye. Stop the silk and the dubbing process just 2 or 3 mms behind the eye. Now take the strip of bear's skin, and tie in by its tip on top of the hook shank just behind the eye at the point where the silk is now hanging at anchor. Make sure that the natural lie of the hair is flowing in the direction of the bend of the hook.

The strip of skin is now drawn tight over the back of the seal's fur body, and secured in position with one firm turn of the oval tinsel which is taken carefully through the hair and down onto the skin without trapping down any of the individual hairs. The tinsel is then continued in this manner all the way back to the anchored silk, making five or six equally spaced turns through the hair. On reaching the silk, tie the tinsel off and cut away the waste. All that remains to complete the lure is to form a neat head with the tying silk, whip finish and varnish.

Black Chenille

There are few better ways of starting the season than by using a black lure, and one that has stood the test of time and is immensely versatile is the Black Chenille. Fished from the bank with a medium sinking line or shooting head with a slow or steady retrieve, it should get most early season anglers off the mark. A variation in blustery conditions is to pinch a lead shot or substitute on the line just in front of the Black Chenille's head, and with a floating line and long leader allow the cross wind to bump your line and, therefore, your fly enticingly up and down as it swings round.

Bob Church invented the lure in 1971 to fish Draycote Water where brown trout autopsies showed they were feeding on the countless caddis grubs using black straw for their cases from the erstwhile corn field which was Biggin Bay. The use of chenille in the dressing was novel for British fly patterns at the time. The technique was to use a size 6 Black Chenille in conjunction with a lead core line and fish very deep from a boat. It produced for Bob a series of heavyweight bag limits at Draycote.

Anglers have since found the Black Chenille a great all-rounder, and Bob himself regards it as an all-season lure. Another of his methods in late April when myriads of black buzzers appear is to use a sink tip line or shooting head and with a steady retrieve present the lure a foot or so below the surface where the midge pupae are prevalent.

Time and again on all types of water, a Black Chenille whipped back through the surface fast or with a series of short, sharp pulls on a floating line in the last twenty minutes before dusk will complete a bag limit. Trout will frequently grab it with gusto even though seemingly interested only in caenis, midges or black smut.

It is advisable to stock all sizes from 6 to 10, and even a few tandem lures on 6's or 8's for fishing deep.

How to tie

Hook:	L/S 6–10
Silk:	Black
Body:	Black chenille
Rib:	Flat silver tinsel
Tail:	Black hackle fibres
Wing:	Four matching black cock hackle feathers
Throat hackle:	Black hackle fibres

Run waxed silk from immediately behind the eye of the hook, down the shank in neat, butting turns and stop opposite the point of the hook. Next, take a fairly generous bunch of black cock hackle fibres and tie in on top of the shank to form the tail. Continue with the silk down the shank in neat, butting turns, lashing down the tail fibres as you go, and stop just before the bend begins.

With your very first turn of the tying silk returning up the shank, catch in a short length of flat silver tinsel. With your second turn of the tying silk, catch in a length of black chenille by its stripped central core. Now continue with the silk back up the shank in neat, butting turns, lashing down the butt ends of the tinsel, chenille core and tail fibres as you go. Stop a short distance from the eye, leaving room for the hackle and wing, and let the silk hang at anchor.

Next, wind the chenille up the shank in neat, butting turns and, on reaching the silk, tie off with three or four firm turns. Cut away the waste chenille. The ribbing is now wound over the chenille body in tight, evenly spaced turns, and tied off on reaching the anchored silk. After cutting away the waste tinsel, cover the raw end and that of the chenille with firm turns of the silk, and in so doing prepare a level bed on which to tie the beard hackle and wing.

Now turn the hook over in the vice and tie in a generous bunch of black cock hackle fibres to form the beard hackle, then, after cutting away the waste ends, turn the hook back to its original position ready to receive the wing.

For the wing, select four matching cock hackles that have a nice dense central list, and place each pair tip on tip, one on top of the other. The two pairs of matched hackles can then themselves be paired up by placing them tip on tip, back to back (concave on concave). The four feathers are now gripped tightly in this position while the unwanted flue and fibres are stripped away to expose the central stems, and at the same time reducing the wing to the required length.

The wing can now be offered up and tied in by lashing the four exposed stems firmly on top of the hook shank. It is important that the commencement of the wing fibres is positioned immediately above the beginning of the throat hackle, and that the wing lies in line with, and at ninety degrees to the shank. Once lashed firmly into position, crop away the waste hackle stems which protrude beyond the eye, form a neat head with the tying silk, whip finish and varnish the head.

Black Ghost

This is a streamer pattern of American origin used by fishermen all over the world, and is, in my view, one of the most versatile lures that an angler can have in his box. Basically a fry imitation, it will work at all times of the season but particularly early on. It has taken fish for me on the bigger reservoirs fished deeply and slowly, and has worked equally on smaller fisheries like Rockbourne and Croxley Hall Waters on a floating line and long leader, allowing a reasonable period for it to sink. If you have a number of taps on a slow retrieve, speed it up to steady for fish to take. With this fly, fish often respond to a slow draw up through the water near the end of the retrieve.

In high summer when trout are beating up shoals of minnows or fry, a Black Ghost fished slowly on a long leader and floating line in the path or vicinity of marauding fish will often produce savage takes so use monofilament of at least 5 lb breaking strain.

How to tie

Hook:	L/S 6–10
Silk:	Black
Tail:	Golden pheasant crest
Rib:	Flat silver tinsel
Body:	Black floss or wool
Wings:	Four white cock hackles
Throat hackle:	Golden pheasant crest
Shoulders:	Jungle cock or substitute
Head:	Black varnish

Run waxed silk from immediately behind the eye of the hook, down the shank in neat, butting turns and stop at a position opposite the point of the hook. Now take a golden pheasant crest feather and prepare it for tying in by stripping away any insignificant fibres from its base. The crest feather can now be tied in on top of the shank with the natural curve of the feather sweeping upwards. Continue with the silk down the shank in neat, butting turns, lashing down the tail feather as you go, and stop at a point just before the start of the bend. It is always important to hold all tails in place whilst being tied down, but with golden pheasant crest feathers it is essential to carry this out diligently because of their unruly nature.

With your very first turn of the tying silk returning up the shank, catch in a length of medium width number 3 or 4 flat silver tinsel and then continue up the shank in neat, butting turns, lashing down the raw end of the tinsel as you go. Stop the silk a short distance from the eye of the hook, leaving just enough space for the throat hackle and wing. Now for the body.

My favourite way of forming a neat floss body is to take a length of Pearsall's marabou floss silk and separate the plies into two equal halves. Having done this, take hold of one of the separated strands of floss and tie in at the position where the silk is now hanging at anchor. The strand of floss is then wound down the shank to the commencement of the tail, and then back again to the anchored silk where it is tied off and the waste cut away. Now take hold of the tinsel and rib the body with firm, open spirals. On reaching the silk, tie the tinsel down and cut away the waste. The raw ends of the floss and tinsel can now be covered with firm turns of the tying silk which is then returned to the head end of the body ready to receive the beard hackle.

Turn the hook over in the vice and then select one, or in some cases two, golden pheasant crest feathers which will form the throat hackle. Prepare the crest feathers as you did for the tail feather, and then tie in as one would a normal beard hackle. After tying in, cut away the waste fibres and cover their butts with firm turns of the silk. The hook can now be returned to its original position in the vice.

Now select four matching white cock hackles for the wing. Place each pair tip on tip, one on top of the other. The two pairs of matched hackles can then themselves be paired up by placing them tip on tip, back to back. The four feathers are now gripped tightly in this position while the unwanted base flue and fibres are stripped away, at the same time reducing the wing to its required length.

The wing can now be offered up and tied in by lashing the four exposed stems firmly on top of the hook shank. It is important that the commencement of the wing fibres is positioned immediately above that of the throat hackle. Make four or five firm turns of the silk travelling in the direction of the hook eye before cropping away the waste hackle stems at a shallow angle to the shank. Continue with the silk in very firm, butting turns until the cropped ends of the hackle stems have been covered, and then return it to where the wing begins. Two jungle cock feathers are now positioned one on either side of the wing, and secured there with touching turns of the tying silk travelling towards the eye of the hook. Just before the eye is reached, snip away any vestige of the jungle cock stems that may remain, cover their ends and whip finish. Two coats of cellire varnish will complete the lure.

Black Lure

Black is the most commonly used colour for early and late season fishing on the big reservoirs, and though many black flies are now available, the Black Lure was probably the prototype. Fished very deeply and slowly from a boat with a lead impregnated line or an aquasink it will take big fish at waters like Grafham and Rutland. It can also be retrieved much more quickly when it probably arouses the aggressive instincts of trout. One of its disadvantages is that sometimes it has the annoying habit of tangling its wing feathers in the bend of the hook after constant casting. Tandem lures are costly to buy in the shops as the making of the mounts is a time-consuming process, so it is well worth while to acquire Bob's method of assembling them.

How to tie

Hook:	L/S 6–12, tied in tandem, two or more
Silk:	Black
Ribs:	Oval or fine flat silver tinsel

34

Bodies:	Black floss
Wings:	Two or four black cock or hen hackles, tied back to back
Hackle:	Black cock or hen or none

In order to avoid unnecessary repetition, I think at this point we must place the Badger Lure, the Black Lure and the White Lure all in the same category, because the assembly of the mounts and the way in which they are dressed are identical to one another, and it is only the individual materials which really set them apart. So please use the assembly and tying sequence as already described for the Badger Lure on page 15 in conjunction with the materials outlined below.

Blithfield Rabbit

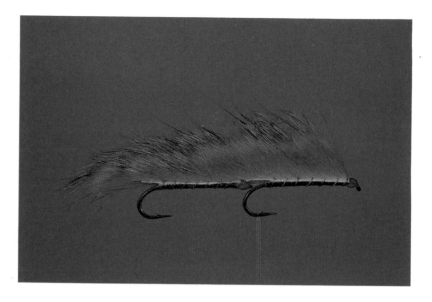

The virtues of rabbit as a winging material have recently been expounded by Bev Harper Smith. Whilst marabou feather fibres, when drawn through the water, tend to hold together by their barbs, the individual rabbit hairs remain separate. Not only does each filament move, but together they produce an aura of iridescence.

Steve Parton tells me that the Blithfield Rabbit, which utilises rabbit pelt, has been in use for over ten years at Blithfield Reservoir. It was originally developed by several of the season ticket holders to deal with perch fry in the terminal stages of perch ulcer disease. It has proved to be a deadly lure for fishing immediately sub-surface in conjunction with floating and intermediate density lines. It can also be highly effective for fishing very slowly at a great depth.

Now that Bev Harper Smith has introduced a variety of colours of soft tanned rabbit, this has widened the possibilities for the use of other colour combinations including black and silver, and chinchilla and gold. Steve also mentioned to me that Hot Orange and Gold Rabbits have proved to work well fished fairly slowly when rainbows are feeding on daphnia.

How to tie

Hook:	Two L/S 2–4 in tandem
Monofilament linkage:	A single strand of 30–40 lb nylon monofilament; or a double strand of extra stiff 12 lb Tynex monofilament
Silk:	Red
Body:	One twenty-fifth gold lurex
Rib:	Fine oval gold
Wing:	Strip of rabbit fur on skin, continuous along both hook shanks, and tied down matuka style
Head:	Red varnish

Start by removing the eye from what will be the rear hook of the tandem mount. This operation is completely optional, but I like to do so because it gives a more streamlined and professional appearance. To remove the hook eye, simply bury the hook deep into the vice with just the eye left protruding. The eye is then gripped with a pair of pliers or strong forceps, and cracked smartly backwards.

Having prepared the rear hook, place it in the vice in the normal way, and then run the waxed silk from close to the end down the shank in neat, butting turns, and stop at a position opposite the point. Now catch in a 10 cm length of number 14 or 16 oval gold before continuing on down the shank, again in neat, butting turns, and lashing down the gold tinsel as you go to stop just before the bend begins. Because there will be no separate tail to this lure and the fact that the gold body should be kept as level as possible, the nylon mount is attached in a slightly different way from that described for the Alexandra Demon.

With the silk now hanging at anchor at the bend of the hook, take 14 cms of 12 lb Tynex, double it, and then offer it up, and tie in on top of the shank with the loose ends facing forwards. Make four or five very firm turns of the silk around the shank and monofilament strands, travelling in the direction of the eye. The next job is to pull the loop of monofilament tight up to the initial whipping before moving on any further. This done, take a tube of superglue, and apply a little along the length of the two strands of monofilament, including the four or five whippings of silk. The amount of glue used should be just enough to run between the strands and onto the top of the hook shank. After applying the glue, quickly continue lashing the monofilament to the top of the shank with firm, butting turns of the silk. Stop the silk 4 or 5 mms from the end of the hook. A single strand of heavy monofilament may be attached in the same way as described for the double strand, but it is advisable to crimp the portion of nylon which will be whipped to the shank. This is quick and easy to do using a pair of toothed pliers or heavy forceps.

Now take about 30 cms of gold lurex, the length of which will vary depending on the hook size you are using, and tie in with three or four forward turns of the silk. The lurex is then wound down the shank in neat, butting turns, and then back again to the tying silk, whereupon it is tied off and the waste cut away. The silk is now secured in place with a two or three turn whip finish, and then left to hang free while the front hook is dressed up to this same stage. This length of silk will later be used to secure the rabbit's fur back of the lure.

The rear hook is now removed from the vice and replaced by another of the same size, this time complete with eye. As before, introduce the tying silk just behind the eye of the hook, and then run it in neat, butting turns down the shank, and stop opposite the point of the hook. The rest of the dressing for the front hook, namely the tying in of the oval gold, the lashing of the monofilament strands to the shank and the dressing of the gold body, is identical to that already described for the rear hook. So let us now pick up the dressing where the rabbit wing or back is about to be prepared and tied in.

Lay a piece of rabbit pelt, fur downwards, on a wooden board or thick cardboard, and then slice away a 2 to 3 mm width strip with the aid of a straight edge and scalpel. The minimum length of the strip with skin attached should be long enough to overhang the eye of the front hook and the bend of the rear hook by at least $1\frac{1}{2}$ to 2 cms. This will give you something to hold and pull on while the strip is being secured in place.

It makes little difference on which hook the strip is first secured, but I prefer to start in the middle of the strip and secure it to the front hook first. In order to do this, leave the front hook securely locked in the vice, and then position the fur centrally over the back (top) of the mount. The oval gold which has been left to hang at the rear of this hook is now brought round and over the top of the shank, passing carefully through the crest of the fur, and then down the other side. This process is repeated in firm, equally spaced turns until the anchored silk, positioned just behind the eye, is reached. At this point, tie the tinsel down and cut away the waste. The excess strip of fur which overhangs the eye can also be trimmed away, and a neat head formed with the tying silk before whip finishing and cutting away the waste silk. The rear hook can now be placed back into the vice, and the remainder of the strip of fur secured to the top of the shank in exactly the same manner as was the front hook. When the time comes to tie the oval tinsel off and whip finish, remember to form a large enough loop to enable the silk to pass around the front hook.

All that remains now to finish the lure is to trim away the excess strip of fur at the rear of the hook, level with the bend, and to varnish the two silk whippings.

The Blue and Silver Terror

Here is another three hook lure perhaps destined for renewed popularity now that lead-lining and other forms of deepwater fishing are more common, especially in early season. James Hardy of the House of Hardy tells me that The Blue and Silver Terror first appeared in their catalogues as early as 1908 as a lure for sea trout, but also claimed to be useful for freshwater lochs. Its price, incidentally, at that time was 5d! Bob recommends its use in bright, cold conditions particularly if the water is clear.

How to tie

Hooks:	Three size 8 or 10 standard shanks, tied in tandem with the middle hook facing upwards
Monofilament mount:	A double strand of stiff 12 lb Tynex is ideal
Silk:	Black
Tails:	Scarlet or crimson floss or fine wool. DF materials

	such as Datam glo-brite numbers three or four and
	DRF fire-orange nylon floss are very useful
Body:	Flat silver tinsel
Rib:	Fine silver wire
Wing:	Four matching cock hackles, dyed bright blue
Overwing:	Two slips of silver mallard flank feather

The forming of the mount and the tying in of the tails, bodies and beard hackle is performed in exactly the same way as for the Alexandra Demon on page 5. So, to avoid unnecessary repetition, let us pick up the dressing sequence at the point where the lure is ready to receive its wings.

For the wing, select four matching bright blue cock hackles. Place each pair tip on tip, one on top of the other. This done, the two pairs of matching hackles can then themselves be paired up by placing tip on tip, back to back. The four feathers are now gripped tightly in this position whilst the unwanted base flue and fibres are stripped away, so reducing the wing to its required length.

The wing can now be offered up and tied in by lashing the four exposed stems firmly on top of the hook shank. It is important that the commencement of the wing fibres is positioned immediately above that of the throat hackle. Make four or five firm turns of the silk travelling in the direction of the hook eye before cropping away the waste hackle stems at a shallow angle to the shank. Continue with the silk in very firm, butting turns until the cropped ends of the hackle stems have been covered, and then return it to the commencement of the wing. We are now ready for the overwing.

Select two large, matching silver mallard flank feathers and take a fairly broad slip from each. The slips should come from opposing sides as in normal webbed fibre winging procedure. Having removed the matching slips, they are then offered up for tying in. This is done by laying one on either side of the streamer hackle wing, positioning them so that their upper edges come into line with the uppermost edge of the wing. As soon as both slips are in position, they are held there with the finger and thumb of the left hand whilst two or three light pinch and loop lashings are made to secure them. These initial loops must be administered lightly, otherwise the delicate slips are liable to distort. Now remove the grip to check that all has gone well. If it has, re-establish the grip on the wing just to steady it, and then continue to secure the slips with much firmer, butting turns of the silk travelling in the direction of the hook eye. When approximately halfway back to the eye, the waste ends of the slips can be trimmed away, and their raw ends covered with more touching turns of the silk. Just before the eye is reached, finish the head off with the usual whip finish. Two coats of cellire varnish will complete the lure.

Bobby Dazzle Lure

This fly was tied by Jim Clements, Steve Parton's boat partner, to imitate perch fry at Blithfield, and makes use of silver Bobby Dazzle material for the body. This is a braided tape which is much easier to work than mylar, and gives subtly iridescent effects. The tail is shorter than on a Sid Knight Dog Nobbler and it contains strands of pearl flashabou.

Jim has been using the lure with great success at Blithfield since the 1985 season. Off the bank, he fishes it on a slow sink shooting head, and just twitches it along the bottom. He uses yellow stren as backing line, and watches the dip in it as an indication of a take with the rod tip about two feet above the water retrieving his line very slowly. Jim says you soon know which is a take and which the bottom.

He has had some very good days fishing the Bobby Dazzle Lure from a boat at anchor. He generally fishes into the dam or causeway in the same manner as from the bank but with a faster sinking line like a Wet Cel 11 or an aquasink, and still watching his yellow stren as an indicator.

His other method is to utilise a stern quarter drogue, and, as the boat moves, to cast more or less straight in front so that he can cover a lot of water and, by changing to different lines, fish varied depths. This is a very deadly method when fish are feeding on fry.

Jim not only sent me some sample flies, but also the material so that I could tie some up for myself. He uses white dacron for the underbody.

How to tie

Hook:	L/S 6–8 cranked to take a BB shot
Silk:	White
Tail:	White marabou with four to six strands of pearl flashabou intermingled
Underbody:	White dacron but not required if white silk is used
Body:	Silver Bobby Dazzle material
Rib:	Oval silver
Hackle:	Palmered grizzle

The mount for this lure, that is the hook with **BB** shot attached, is constructed in exactly the same way as are the rest of the Dog Nobbler series, but with one minor difference. The hook shank close to the eye is cranked downwards.

Take the prepared mount, and place it in the vice, taking care to mask the point below the level of the jaws. Now run the waxed silk from immediately behind the lead head down the shank in neat, butting turns, and stop at a position opposite the point. A short 10 cm length of oval silver tinsel is now caught in at this position, and the silk then continued on down the shank in neat, butting turns, lashing down the tinsel as you go. Stop the silk just before the bend begins.

The silk is then returned back up the shank in firm, open turns, to stop fractionally behind the lead head. Now take a generous plume of white marabou fibres into which four, five or six pearl flashabou strands have been intermingled, and spin into a shuttlecock formation as described in the tying of the Cat's Whisker on page 50. The plume can then be tied in on top of the shank by the tip of the rolled butts, and lashed firmly into place with neat, butting turns travelling down the shank. Stop the silk on reaching the last laps of the foundation whippings. The silk can now be returned back up the shank in firm, open turns to stop once again just behind the lead head. The length of tail to aim for should be slightly longer than the overall length of the hook being used. For a size 8 L/S this would be approximately $3\frac{1}{2}$ cms.

Now take a 10 to 12 cm length of silver Bobby Dazzle material, and catch it in with three or four firm turns of the tying silk just behind the lead head. The Bobby Dazzle material can then be wound down the shank in neat, touching turns as far as the start of the tail, and then back again in the same manner. On reaching the anchored silk, tie the Bobby Dazzle material off and cut away the waste. The raw ends of this material are then covered with firm turns of the silk which is then returned to the head end of the body ready to receive the grizzle hackle.

Select a well marked cock grizzle hackle which is long in fibre and overall length, and strip away all the base flue to leave the central stem exposed. The hackle is then tied in by its stem, and wound in firm, equally spaced turns down the body until the start of the tail is reached. At this point, the hackle pliers change hands whilst the oval silver is wound up and over the body to trap down and hold firm the last turn of the palmered hackle. The hackle pliers can then be released, and the remainder of the body and hackle ribbed firmly with the tinsel in open and equally spaced turns. During the ribbing process, avoid trapping down the hackle fibres with the tinsel. On reaching the anchored silk, tie the tinsel off and cut away the waste. All that remains is to cover the waste end of the tinsel with turns of the tying silk, and whip finish. Any surplus grizzle hackle at the rear of the hook can now be trimmed away, and the laps of silk immediately behind the lead head clear varnished.

Breatherliser

At Chew Valley Lake from August onwards minnows, sticklebacks and fry congregate in their thousands in the sheltered bays. Every so often there is a silvery scattering of myriads of little fish as a predatory trout, fattening up for the autumn, scythes through their ranks. The Breatherliser is an early British streamer lure based on Canadian models devised by Alec Iles in the 1960s to imitate such little fish at Chew. He took good bags of trout by retrieving it quickly when, no doubt, the hot orange wing feathers aroused the aggressive instincts of the rainbows. I have been more successful on that water by fishing lures like the Breatherliser very slowly with an occasional draw. This way they are often taken with a satisfying thump.

How to tie

Hook:	L/S 6–8
Silk:	Black
Tail:	Fibres from a soft black cock or hen hackle

Body:	Flat silver tinsel. If lurex is used it is essential that a ribbing of fine silver wire is also applied
Wings:	Two hot-orange cock hackles with two Green Highlander hackles outside, streamer fashion
Eyes:	Jungle cock or substitute
Hackle:	Badger wound as a collar
Head:	Black varnish

Run waxed silk from immediately behind the eye of the hook, down the shank in neat, butting turns and stop at a position opposite the point. Now take a soft cock hackle feather and strip away a bunch of fibres taking care to keep their tips in line. The bunch of fibres is now offered up and tied in on top of the shank to form the tail of the lure, after which the silk is continued down the shank in neat, butting turns, lashing down the tail fibres as you go. Stop the silk just before the bend of the hook begins.

If a silver wire rib is to be used, then this is now caught in with your very first turn of the tying silk returning up the shank. Continue up the shank with the silk in neat, butting turns, lashing down the butt end of the silver wire and the remnants of the tail fibres as you go, and stop a short distance from the eye, allowing just enough space for the wings and collar hackle.

The flat silver tinsel, or lurex if you prefer it, can now be tied in and wound down the shank in neat, touching turns to the tail, then back again. On reaching the anchored silk, tie the tinsel off and cut away the waste. The tinsel or lurex body can now be ribbed with tight, equally spaced turns of the silver wire. On reaching the silk, tie off and cut away the waste wire. The raw ends of the tinsel and waste wire can now be covered with touching turns of the tying silk which is then returned to the head end of the body.

We are now ready for the wings. Select four matching cock hackles, two dyed hot-orange, and two dyed Green Highlander, and pair them up by laying one Green Highlander on top of a hot-orange. Lay them concave on convex, and tip on tip. Having prepared both sets of hackles in this manner, they themselves can then be paired up. This is done by placing the two pairs tip on tip, and back to back (concave on concave). Grip the feathers tightly in this position while all the base flue and sufficient fibres are stripped away to leave the overall length of the hackles exactly right for the finished wing. The wing can now be offered up and tied in on top of the hook shank by lashing the stripped stems firmly with four or five turns of the silk travelling in the direction of the eye. The excess stems can now be cropped away at a shallow angle to the shank and their butts covered with very firm turns of silk which is then returned to the commencement of the wing.

The two jungle cock eyes can how be prepared and tied in. To do this, select two matching eye feathers and strip away the unwanted flue and superfluous fibres from below the eye. This done, position one eye feather on either side of the streamer wing and secure in place with several turns of the silk. Do not take the silk any further at present, but instead return it to the start of the wing, and there tie in a prepared badger cock hackle by its stripped stem. The silk can now be taken forward towards the eye in neat, touching turns, lashing down the hackle stem and jungle cock as you go. About halfway back to the eye, the waste ends of the hackle stems and jungle cock can be trimmed away and their raw ends covered with the silk. Now take hold of the tip of the hackle in the hackle pliers and make four full turns around the hook shank, each one in front of the other. The hackle can now be tied off and the waste cut away. All that remains is to give the hackle a nice swept back appearance. This is achieved by sweeping the hackle fibres backwards with the first two fingers and thumb of the left hand, and covering their roots with two or three turns of the silk, after which a neat head is formed with the tying silk and finished off with the usual whip finish. Two coats of cellire will complete the lure.

Cat's Whisker

When Bob Church states that he has been more impressed by a lure than any other artificial he has ever tried, then any fisherman has to consider seriously including it in his fly box. David Train who invented the Cat's Whisker developed it originally from a tadpole-type lure with a yellow chenille body and a white marabou tail. When he found that at times fish tended to take the tail only, he modified the fly by adding a wing of white marabou stiffened to prevent it looping around the hook bend by a small bunch of white cat's stiff whiskers. Hence the name Cat's Whiskers. He then added bath chain bead eyes to improve the looks and help the lure swim when retrieved on a more even keel.

He and Bob Church have had very considerable successes with the fly on a number of waters. It is highly visible to the angler, and David Train says that the first indication of a take sometimes is the disappearance of the glowing white blob like a light being switched off. Bob Church tells me that not only does it work well on a fast sinker in early or late season cold conditions, but he found to his amazement that it was also brilliantly effective on floating or slow sink lines in the summer. It should be fished as a single fly on a long leader of about 4 metres. Fine nylon can be used if you have no white cat at your house. Bob Church uses nothing.

How to tie

Hook:	L/S 6 bronze
Silk:	Black
Tail:	White marabou, generous
Body:	Yellow fluorescent chenille
Wing:	White marabou, generous
Eyes:	Bath chain bead eyes
Head:	Black varnish
Rib:	Fine oval silver (optional)

Run waxed silk from immediately behind the eye of the hook, down the shank in neat, butting turns, and stop just before the start of the bend. The silk is now returned back up the shank in firm, open spirals to a position approximately 3 mm behind the eye. This bed of tying silk will act as a non-slip base on which the marabou tail and, eventually, the wing will be tied.

For the tail you will require a marabou feather that has quite long fibres at least three times the hook length. Having selected such a feather, strip away several sections of the fibres and lay them tip on tip to form a generous plume. This done, pick up the plume and measure it for length against the hook. What you are aiming for is a tail that will overhang the bend of the hook which is equivalent in length to almost two hook lengths. In addition to this, there also needs to be almost another hook's length of marabou with which to tie in the plume.

Having measured the plume and cropped away the excess material from the butt end, the portion of the plume which is to be tied in along the shank should first be moistened with saliva and then rolled tightly between finger and thumb of the right hand whilst simultaneously releasing the grip of the left hand to allow the spray of fibres to rotate. This spinning action should be continued until the butts are fully compressed and locked together. Done correctly, the fibres will now resemble a little shuttlecock and can be dropped onto the fly tying bench without fear of their breaking apart. The plume can now be offered up and tied in on top of the hook shank by the tip of the rolled butts, and then lashed firmly into place with butting turns of the silk travelling back towards the bend. As soon as the end of the foundation laps of tying silk is reached, the tying down of the plume can stop.

With your very first turn of the tying silk returning up the shank, catch in a length of fine oval silver tinsel, if desired, and with your second turn catch in a length of yellow chenille by its stripped central core. Continue with the silk up the shank in firm, butting turns, tying down the raw ends of the tinsel and chenille as you go, and stop approximately 3 mm behind the eye. The chenille can how be wound up the shank in firm, butting turns, and on reaching the silk, tied off with three firm turns of the silk. The waste chenille can then be cut away. Now take hold of the silver tinsel, if used, and rib the chenille body with firm open spirals. On reaching the anchored silk, tie the tinsel off, cut away the waste, and then cover the butt ends with the silk before returning it to the head end of the body.

We are now ready for the wing which is formed in exactly the same way as was the tail, but this time it is to be slightly shorter. The length to aim for is approximately one and a half times the length of the hook. Having formed the plume, it can now be tied in on top of the hook shank close up to the head end of the body. The waste butts are then cropped away and their raw ends covered with firm turns of the silk which, at the same time, is forming a firm, level bed on which the chain bead eyes are to be tied.

Now take a length of bead-type bath chain and snip away two beads that are still attached to each other by the short link. The eyes are then positioned on top of the shank, immediately behind the eye of the hook, and then lashed firmly into place with several figure-of-eight lashings. I find it a good idea to add a spot of superglue after the first two or three lashings and then continue the tying down through the glue. Finish the lure off with the usual whip finish, but in this case behind the bead chain eyes as opposed to behind the hook eye. A touch of black varnish over the whippings will complete the lure.

Chief Needabeh

This is one of those beautiful gaudy flies which Taff Price says is worth having in your box to provoke trout into rising for what he calls "an anger take". The Americans are far more adventurous and inventive in the realms of streamers and bucktails than we are, and this lure is named after a real Red Indian chief. I always carry a couple in my box to resort to on those desperate days, usually hot, sunny and windless. Then I use a long leader treated to sink, with a floating line or a sink tip, and retrieve at good speed right in to my feet or the side of the boat. Usually nothing happens, but occasionally a bow wave appears behind my fly and bang! You're into a rainbow. Orange often seems to have a fascination for rainbows, especially when daphnia is about, and Chief Needabeh has outside wings of orange cock hackle.

How to tie

Hook:	L/S 6–10
Silk:	Black

Tag:	Oval silver tinsel
Body:	Scarlet floss silk
Rib:	Oval silver tinsel
Wings:	Two yellow cock hackles back to back, and two orange cock hackles outside
Shoulders:	Jungle cock or substitute
Hackle:	Mixed yellow and scarlet cock
Head:	Black varnish

Run waxed silk from immediately behind the eye of the hook, down the shank in neat, butting turns, and stop a short distance from where the bend begins. Now take a short length of number 14 oval silver tinsel and catch it in by its tip on the side of the shank facing you. The silk is now wound in neat, butting turns up to the start of the bend, lashing down the tinsel as you go, and then returned to the spot where the tinsel was first trapped in. The tag can now be formed by winding the tinsel in touching turns up the shank; about five to seven turns, depending on hook size, will suffice. When sufficient turns have been made, tie the tinsel off with three firm turns of the silk, and then cut away the waste. This same piece of tinsel can now be tied in again on the side of the shank and lashed firmly into place with turns of the silk working back towards the head end of the tag. This will later be used to rib the body of the lure. The silk can now be taken back up the shank in neat, butting turns, and stopped a short distance from the eye, allowing just enough space for the wing and hackle.

A length of scarlet floss is now tied in at this point, and then wound down the shank in neat, touching turns until it comes flush up to the head end of the tag. The floss is then returned back up the shank, again in neat, butting turns, and, on reaching the anchored silk, tied off with three firm turns and the waste cut away. This is then followed by the oval tinsel which is wound in firm, open and equally spaced turns until the silk is reached, whereupon it is tied off and the waste cut away. The butt ends of the tinsel and floss are now covered with firm turns of the silk which is then returned to the head end of the body ready to receive the wing.

For the wing, select four matching cock hackles, two dyed yellow and two dyed orange, and pair them up by laying one orange on top of a yellow. Lay them concave on convex, and tip on tip. Having prepared both sets of hackles in this manner, they themselves can then be paired up. This is done by placing the two pairs tip on tip, and back to back (concave on concave). Grip the feathers tightly in this position while all the base flue and sufficient fibres are stripped away to leave the overall length of the hackles exactly right for the finished wing. The wing can now be offered up, and tied in by lashing the stripped stems firmly into place on top of the shank with four or five turns of the silk travelling in the direction of the eye. The excess stems can now be cropped away at a shallow angle to the shank, and their butts covered with further firm turns of the silk which is then returned to the commencement of the wing.

The two jungle cock eyes can now be prepared and tied in. Select two matching eye feathers, and strip away the unwanted flue and superfluous fibres from below the eye. Now position one eye feather on either side of the streamer wing, and secure in place with several turns of the silk. Do not take the silk any further forward at present, but instead return it to the start of the wing, and there tie in the red and yellow hackles which will form the mixed collar hackle. The two hackles should be paired up and tied in as one. The silk can now be taken forward towards the eye in neat, touching turns, lashing down the hackle stems and the jungle cock as you go. About halfway back to the eye, the waste ends of the hackle stems and jungle cock can be trimmed away and their raw ends covered with the silk. Now take hold of the two hackle tips in the jaws of the hackle pliers and wind them together as one. Make two or three full turns around the shank, one in front of the other, then tie off and cut away their waste ends. All that remains is to give the hackle fibres a nice backwards rake. This is done by sweeping the hackle fibres backwards with the fingers and thumb of the left hand whilst covering their roots with several turns of the silk. A neat head is then formed with the tying silk and whip finished. Two coats of cellire will complete the lure.

Christmas Tree

Surprisingly, marabou has been around for at least twenty-five years which is how long Tom Saville of Nottingham has stocked it, but it was not until 1973 that Bob Church popularised it with the Appetiser and, later, Jack Frost. The Christmas Tree is another lure of that breed, originated by Les Lewis, and has been a great favourite at Rutland Water ever since it opened. It is worth bearing in mind that the fibres of the plumes of marabou are very fragile, so be careful when you are unhooking fish by holding the body or the bend of the hook if you want your lure to last for more than the one fish.

Christmas Tree is fundamentally a black marabou lure, but with a fluorescent green tail and a red fluorescent collar. It is a versatile fly which can be fished at any depth or speed, but to get the best action out of marabou it must be fished slowly.

How to tie

Hook: L/S 6–10
Silk: Black

55

Tail:	Fluorescent green wool or floss
Rib:	Oval silver tinsel
Body:	Black chenille
Wing:	Generous spray of black marabou
Collar:	Red fluorescent wool or floss

Run waxed silk from immediately behind the eye of the hook down the shank in neat, butting turns, and stop approximately one third of the way down the shank from the eye. Now take a short length of DF green wool or floss of approximately 4 cms, and tie in on top of the shank at this position. This will later form the tail of the lure. The silk can then be continued down the shank in very firm, neat, butting turns, lashing down the wool to the shank as you go. It is important that the wool is drawn tightly during this tying down process, and kept in place on top of the shank.

With your very first turn of the tying silk returning up the shank, catch in a length of flat silver tinsel, and, with your second turn, a length of black chenille by its stripped central core. The silk is now returned up the shank in neat, butting turns, lashing down the raw ends of the tinsel and chenille as you go. Stop the silk a short distance from the eye allowing just enough space for the wing and throat material. The chenille can now be wound along the shank in neat, butting turns until the anchored silk is reached, and then tied off with three firm turns of the silk. The waste chenille can then be cut away. Now take hold of the tinsel, rib the chenille body with firm, open spirals, and, on reaching the anchored silk, tie the tinsel off and cut away the waste. The raw ends of the tinsel and chenille can now be covered with firm turns of the silk which is then returned to the head end of the body.

The DF wool or floss tail can now be cropped to length and flared out. This is done by taking hold of the excess wool as it hangs to the rear of the bend, and pulling it tight in line with the shank. Now lay opened scissors across the taut wool, measure the tail for length, and then crop away with one crisp, clean cut. The individual fibres of the tail are now flared out using either the point of the dubbing needle or the two points of a pair of partially opened, fine pointed fly tying scissors in much the same way as one would use a comb.

The hook can now be turned over in the vice ready to receive the throat collar. The usual material for the collar of this lure is wool, but in many cases it proves to be rather bulky in its appearance. However, since the introduction of Datam Glo-brite floss, I have used this versatile material for various things, and for the throat of the Christmas Tree I find it unbeatable. If you decide to use wool, one or two strands, depending on thickness, are lashed in place on top of the reversed hook so that it encompasses the upper one third to one half of the shank. The portion of waste wool between the lashings of tying silk and the eye of the hook can now be trimmed away, and their raw ends covered with firm turns of the silk. This done, the length of the collar can be dealt with in much the same way as was the tail. Pull the material taut, crop to length with one crisp cut, and then flare out the individual fibres as described earlier. If, on the other hand, Glo-brite floss is to be used, then the sequence of tying in is very similar to that already described for the wool collar. The only real difference is the preparation of the Glo-brite floss. Being a single strand floss, it will require multiple doublings in order to give the required thickness for the job in hand. My way of doing this is simply to wrap it around a slightly gaped finger and thumb until the required amount is reached. The opposing ends of the circular formation are then cut through, and the two halves then laid together as one. The rest of the tying in procedure is exactly the same as if wool had been used.

Once the collar has been tied in and cropped to length, the hook can then be returned to its original position in the vice ready to receive the wing. The wing for the Christmas Tree is a generous bunch or spray of black marabou fibres, and it is prepared in the same way as I described for the head and tail plumes of the Cat's Whisker on page 50. So, having prepared the plume of black marbou, it can now be tied in on top of the hook shank immediately above the commencement of the collar. The length of wing to aim for is one that extends just slightly beyond the end of the tail. Having tied the wing in and cropped away the waste butt end at a shallow angle to the shank, the butts can then be covered with firm turns of silk and a neat head formed. Finish the head off with the usual whip finish and two applications of cellire varnish.

Church Fry

A hair wing lure of similar design to the Sweeny Todd introduced by Bob Church as early as 1963 to imitate perch fry at Ravensthorpe Reservoir in Northampton, and publicised initially by Richard Walker. There are times when a lure with a squirrel tail wing will work better than a marabou. When the fly is wet it has a slim profile and it sinks well. Church Fry belongs to that group of orange-based lures like the Whisky Fly which are particularly effective in high July and August temperatures with algae in the water, and rainbows are afflicted by what Bob Church calls "orange madness".

Retrieved very fast, either just below the surface on a floater or in the top six feet on a sink tip or slow sink line, the lure will sometimes produce dramatic interceptions by pursuing fish whose aggressive instincts have been aroused. There are other ways to use it, and Dave Collyer has taken fish deep down using a slow retrieve.

How to tie

Hook:	L/S 6–10
Silk:	Black
Tail:	White feather or hackle fibres
Rib:	Flat gold or silver tinsel
Body:	Orange chenille or fluorescent orange
Wing:	Grey squirrel tail
Throat hackle:	Dyed orange or crimson cock hackle fibres

Run waxed silk from immediately behind the eye of the hook down the shank in neat, butting turns, and stop opposite the point. Now, from a large white cock hackle feather strip away a fairly generous bunch of fibres, taking care to keep their tips in line, and then tie in on top of the hook shank to form the tail of the lure. The silk can now be continued down the shank, still using neat, butting turns, tying down the tail fibres as you go. As with all tails, the position should be maintained on top of the hook shank during the tying down, using gentle pressure and guidance with the finger and thumb of the left hand. Stop the silk just before the bend begins.

With your very first turn of the tying silk returning up the shank, catch in a length of medium width flat silver or gold tinsel, and, with your second turn, a length of orange chenille by its stripped central core. The silk can now be continued up the shank in neat, butting turns, lashing down the butt ends of the tinsel, chenille and tail fibres as you go. Stop the silk a short distance from the head, allowing just enough space for the throat hackle and the wing.

The chenille can now be wound up the shank in neat, butting turns, and, on reaching the anchored silk, tied down with three firm turns of the silk, and then the waste chenille cut away. This is then followed by the tinsel which is wound in firm, open and equally spaced spirals. On reaching the silk, tie the tinsel down with three firm turns of the silk, and then cut away the unwanted tinsel. The raw ends of the chenille and tinsel can now be covered with firm turns of the silk which is then returned to the head end of the body ready to receive the beard hackle. The hook is now turned over in the vice.

For the throat hackle, select a large dyed cock hackle of crimson or orange, and strip away a very generous bunch of fibres, taking care as always to keep their tips in line. The bunch is then offered up, and tied in to form a nice spray around the uppermost portion of the shank. This done, cut away the waste ends of the fibres, and cover their butts with firm turns of the silk. The hook can now be returned to its original position in the vice, and the silk to the head end of the body ready to receive the wing.

The winging procedure for the Church Fry, namely the selection, preparation and tying in of the grey squirrel tail hair, is identical to that already described for the wing of the Banded Squirrel Bucktail on page 18.

Dead Blackbird

Some incredible fish have been taken fishing very deep at the Queen Mother Fishery in West London including a wild $14\frac{1}{2}$ lb brown trout by Dave Wood. One of the great exponents of this type of fishing both at Queen Mother and Farmoor is Mike Peters, the London photographer. When Mike sent me a sample Dead Blackbird, the lure that does all the damage, recently, he suggested it might have been better to send it by parcel post! It is, indeed, five to seven inches long with three hooks arranged at different angles connected with 40 lb nylon, and fished on a leader of at least 12 lb breaking strain. The hooks are offset because most takes come when the lure is travelling upwards, and Mike feels that if you have hooks pointing in different directions it copes with fish attacking from different angles.

Mike's fishing technique is highly specialised and requires an enormous amount of patience, but one season he had twenty-eight brown trout averaging nearly 5 lb with the best at 9 lb 2 oz at Datchet. Every one was caught on a very very slow retrieve (2 inch per second!) using a lead core line and fishing at 70 and 80 feet down. His favourite spots are along the bottom and up the side of fry holding places like dam walls and inlet/outlet towers. Getting the correct depth, he feels, is especially crucial. Mike's final advice for those who wish to try this brand of esoteric fishing is to choose your spot, stick it out, persevere, and ignore all rising fish!

As Bob says, there are no marks for tying a perfect fly, but there may well be some for casting it! On an outing at Farmoor when no one else was catching, Mike took ten browns and rainbows on the Dead Blackbird, this time stripping it along the bottom like a madman. As he said, not fly fishing but fun!

How to tie

Hooks:	Three L/S 8's
Silk:	Black
Linkage:	A single length of 40 lb nylon, or three strands of 12 lb Tynex stiff nylon, plaited
Tail:	Fluorescent green wool, rear hook only, optional
Body:	Large black cock hackle, tied in by its tip at the bend, then twisted together with the tying silk and wound on to form the body
Wings:	Each hook has four black cock hackles for the wing, progressively getting longer from the rear hook to the front
Hackle:	Six turns of a large black cock hackle for each hook

There is little to be gained by giving the full tying instructions for this lure, because basically it is very similar to several of the multi-hook lures described in this book. However, a few words of advice on certain aspects of the Dead Blackbird would not go amiss.

Regarding its general appearance, from the two samples received from Mike Peters, it cannot be over-emphasised that the scruffier this lure is dressed, the better. There are no marks for neat and tidy dressing.

For the monofilament linkage, Mike Peters advocates a six inch length of 40 lb breaking strain nylon with three equally spaced knots over which the hooks are whipped. A good alternative is a length of plaited 12 lb breaking strain stiff Tynex nylon which is available from Tom Savilles of Nottingham. Plaited linkages do not require the above-mentioned knots to ensure a good anchorage. The undulating shape of the plait sees to that.

An easy way to plait nylon is to trap the three strands in the jaws of the fly tying vice, and then plait as normal. Once the required length of plaited linkage is reached, simply give each end – that just outside the jaws of the vice and that held just above the fingers – a dab of Superglue and allow to set. Having done this, the length of plait can be handled freely without the fear of it becoming unwound.

The hackles are wound on after the hackle wings have been tied in. They should be long, and allowed to stand proud. This helps to keep the lure from snagging the bottom.

Dog Nobbler (Sid Knight) – Green Grizzly

The Dog Nobbler was first introduced to the angling scene by Trevor Housby in September 1980, and has since been patented by Sid Knight. Bob has described it as the most deadly lure ever devised which remains within the accepted definition of a trout lure dressing. The principle of a weighted head as used in American "fly rod jigs" was first adapted in this country by Richard Walker in his Leadhead, but the masterstroke by Trevor Housby was the addition of a marabou tail thus combining its delicate mobility with the up and down action of the lead shot.

It has since been developed in a series of colours and palmered versions, and Sid Knight tells me that black, white, yellow and orange are considered the early season attractors with olives, greens and browns for when damselfly nymphs, dragonfly nymphs and stick flies respectively are in the water. The pink version is simply an aggression arouser. Sid picks out the Palmered Eyed White Dog Nobbler as an excellent killer at Rutland.

Bob emphasises that the dressing alone will not produce the desired action from the lure. The retrieve is equally important, the two going hand in hand. Short, sharp draws on the line will make the BB head of the lure rise and fall with each pull and pause of the line, and the tail, like a Chinese streamer, will follow the path of the head faithfully, thus creating rippling undulations which run continually from one end of the tail to the other. And there lies the secret of the Dog Nobbler's success.

How to tie

Hook:	L/S 6
Silk:	Black
Tail:	White marabou, generous
Body:	Fluorescent white chenille
Rib:	Silver wire
Hackle:	Cree cock hackle, dyed olive, tied palmer style, head to tail
Head:	BB split shot secured behind eye of hook with fluorescent yellow eyes and black pupils

Before the actual dressing can begin, the BB split shot must be secured immediately behind the eye of the hook. Sid Knight uses specially angled hook shanks for his commercially dressed patterns in order to guarantee a "non-spin" head, no matter what punishment the lure is given. Mainly for convenience sake, I always use standard straight shank hooks. However, no matter which hook you decide to use, the principles for attaching the shot remain pretty much the same.

I find that deep cut, soft shot are by far the best to use for the construction of the Nobbler, and this is how I attach them. First, open the shot out, using the thumb nails to do so. Then place the shot into the tip of a pair of pliers or strong forceps, and apply just a spot of Superglue into the split. The hook can now be placed into the slit of the shot as close to the eye as possible, making sure that the bend of the hook is presented uppermost. Having positioned the hook shank into the slit of the shot, apply just enough pressure to close the shot tightly together but without flattening it. Once a number of lead heads have been prepared, they can then be given their eyes.

The quickest way of painting eye orbs and pupils is to use a common match stalk. I usually smooth the match first with an emery board just to take off any ragged edges. The tip of the match is then dipped into the paint, and transferred to one side of the lead head by simply lowering the tip until it comes in contact with the lead. Done carefully, the paint will very obligingly leave the match stalk and deposit itself onto the BB shot forming a beautifully round orb as it does so. This process is repeated once more in order to give the head its second eye orb, and then it is put to one side to thoroughly harden off. I use a piece of plastic foam ceiling coving as my drying board. Its shape is ideally suited for the job. Once all the orbs have hardened off, usually the following day, they are then given their pupils, only this time the tip of the match stalk should be slightly finer. Obviously, the pupils are smaller than the orbs. The pupils completed, the hooks are once again set aside until they have dried out.

The rest of the tying is quite simple and straightforward. Start by running waxed silk from immediately behind the lead head down the shank in neat, butting turns, and stop just before the bend is reached. The silk is then returned back up the shank to stop fractionally behind the lead head. Now, take a generous plume of white marabou which has been prepared into the shuttlecock formation already described in the tying of the Cat's Whisker on page 50, and tie in on top of the hook shank by the tip of the rolled butts. The remainder of the rolled butts can now be lashed firmly into place on top of the shank with firm, butting turns of the tying silk travelling back towards the bend. As soon as the end of the foundation laps of tying silk is reached, the tying down of the plume can stop. The length of tail to aim for is about one and a half times the length of the hook being dressed.

With your very first turn of the tying silk returning up the shank, catch in a length of silver wire, and with your second turn a length of white chenille by its stripped central core. Continue with the silk up the shank in neat, butting turns, lashing down the butt ends of the wire and chenille as you go, and stop just behind the lead head. The chenille can now be wound up the shank in neat, butting turns, and, on reaching the anchored silk, tied down and the waste chenille cut away. We are now ready for the body hackle.

Select a dyed olive cree cock hackle which is fairly long in the fibre, and strip away the base flue. The hackle is then tied in by its stripped stem close up to the head, and the waste end cut away. Now grip the tip of the hackle in the jaws of the hackle pliers, and wind it down the chenille body in open, equally spaced turns until the tail is reached. The hackle pliers now change hands whilst the silver wire is brought up and over the body to trap down the stem of the palmered hackle. The hackle pliers can now be disengaged, and the body and palmered hackle ribbed with the wire in firm, open spirals, winding in the opposite direction to that of the hackle. On reaching the anchored silk, tie the wire off and cut away the waste. All that remains is to cover the raw end of the wire with turns of the tying silk, whip finish and add a spot of cellire varnish to the whippings.

Dog Nobbler (Bob Carnill Style)

When Bob says that the Dog Nobbler is the most deadly lure ever invented, he feels that this is doubly so if it happens to be a mini version and tied to the proportions seen in the accompanying photograph. Few anglers realise it, but if the hook length is kept short, and the tail long (three to three and a half times the length of the hook), then the "Devil-Dance", Bob's pet name for the true killing action of the Dog Nobbler, which it produces, operates at its best.

In the springtime, Bob usually fishes the Dog Nobbler from a boat, casting an Aquasink shooting head towards the lee shore. Then, as the weather and water temperature warm up and the trout begin to lift, he will fish the Nobbler on a long leader and weight-forward floating line. However, no matter what line he happens to be using, the retrieve always remains the same short, sharp draw on the line.

One final tip. Whenever you tie on a fresh lure which incorporates marabou in its dressing, always soak it thoroughly by repeatedly squeezing it below the surface of the water before using it. This will allow the marabou to work right from the first cast instead of it

taking several casts and retrieves before it becomes sufficiently wetted
by fishing action alone.

How to tie

Black version

Hook:	Mustad 7780C size 8 standard shank
Silk:	Black
Tail:	Black marabou, very generous, at least three times the length of the hook
Tag:	DRF signal green or phosphor yellow fuzz wool
Body:	Black chenille
Collar hackle:	Black hen or henny cock
Head:	BB split shot with painted eyes

White version

Hook:	Mustad 7780C size 8
Silk:	Red
Tail:	White marabou tied as above
Tag:	As above, optional
Body:	DRF white chenille
Rib:	Medium width flat silver tinsel
Collar hackle:	White or orange hen, or henny cock
Head:	As above

Orange version

Hook:	Mustad 7780C size 8
Silk:	Orange
Tail:	Orange marabou, tied as above
Body:	DRF orange chenille
Collar hackle:	Yellow or hot-orange hen or henny cock
Head:	As above

Yellow version

Hook:	Mustad 7780C size 8
Silk:	Yellow
Tail:	Bright yellow marabou tied as above
Body:	DRF yellow chenille
Collar hackle:	Yellow or hot-orange hen, or henny cock
Head:	As above

The tying sequence for the four Dog Nobblers outlined on p. 69 is basically the same as that already described for Sid Knight's Green Grizzly on page 65. The only differences are: the use of standard shank hooks; the exaggerated proportions of tail to hook length; the addition of a tinsel rib for the White Nobbler; the use of collar hackles as opposed to a palmer hackle; the addition of a small DF tag between the base of the tail and the start of the chenille body. So, to avoid unnecessary repetition, please refer to the Green Grizzly dressing, and make minor adjustments as and when required.

Feather Duster

Bob was first introduced to the Feather Duster in the high summer of 1984 by his good friend, Bob Sharp. They were sharing a boat on Rutland Water, and the conditions were far from conducive to good trout fishing. They were slap bang in the middle of the dog-days and heat wave as well.

The Feather Duster had been taking good trout for Bob Sharp and his regular boat partner throughout the current hard period. Slow and deep had been the secret of their success, and the lure lent itself admirably to this technique. Bob Sharp explained that the beauty of the Duster was that it hardly sinks at all even on the slowest retrieves when it just seems to hover there. And that's how the trout had been wanting it. He later proved his point by taking four good trout in extremely hard conditions, two of which, a rainbow and a brownie, weighed over 4 lb each.

Since then, Bob has used the Duster on numerous occasions and come to know it well. One point still fascinates him, and that is the overall shape of the Duster as it swims through the water as it is completely different from any other lure. He describes it as having the silhouette of a small skimmer bream with the outer edges of the marabou waving enticingly. The takes, too, when it is fished ultra-slowly, are quite unlike those experienced when fishing a lure. At times, they can be so soft as to give the impression that the trout had been sucking the lure instead of attacking it.

In order to present the Duster perfectly, particularly during the dog-days, it is important to anchor the boat, and fish a single lure on the point of a longish leader. A sinking shooting head gives both distance and depth, and also allows for a long, slow and steady retrieve. Strike at any resistance on the line, no matter how slight.

How to tie

Hook:	L/S 6–8
Silk:	Colour to complement the marabou. I use black for black marabou, but red for the white version
Body:	No actual body material involved. However, the butt ends of the tail and body plumes give a fairly substantial covering, colour and texture to the hook shank
Tail and body plumes:	Ten or twelve shuttlecock plumes of spun marabou. Usual colours are all white, black, yellow and orange

Run waxed silk in neat, butting turns from directly behind the eye of the hook down the shank, and stop at a point very slightly round the bend. We are now ready to tie in the first plume which will form the tail of the lure. All ten or twelve plumes which will go into the construction of the Feather Duster are prepared in exactly the same way as was described for the tail and wing of the Cat's Whisker on page 50 so let us assume that these plumes have already been spun into their little shuttlecock formations, and are ready and waiting on the tying bench.

The correct length for the first plume which is to form the tail should be long enough when tied in to extend beyond the bend for a distance which is equivalent to the length of the hook. So take this first plume, and offer it up for tying in. Having measured it for length, secure it firmly on top of the shank with firm turns of the silk travelling towards the eye, and then crop away the waste butt ends. The silk is now taken back to the commencement of the tail ready to tie in the first of the body plumes.

The next plume is now offered up, gauged for length, and then tied in in exactly the same way as the tail plume. After tying in and•cropping away the waste, the silk is again returned to the commencement of the first 'back' plume ready to receive the second. This process is repeated time after time until the eye of the hook is reached, whereupon a neat head is formed with the tying silk and then whip finished. Two coats of cellire will complete the lure.

Though tying of the Duster is simplicity itself, I must warn you, however, that it is both laborious and extremely greedy with marabou. However, the action and the silhouette of the Duster depend entirely on the sheer density of the plumes along its back. Skimp on these and you are defeating the objective. Tied correctly with the plumes densely packed together means that there is no room left even to consider a body for this lure. The main thing is, though, that the trout do not seem to mind in the least.

Frog Nobbler (John Wilshaw)

Another variation of the Dog Nobbler, omitting the lead shot head and replacing it by two layers of lead wire along the length of the hook shank, is called the Frog Nobbler. It received its name from John Wilshaw, formerly editor of Trout Fisherman and Trout and Salmon from when, in 1983, he became the French National stillwater champion. He was using some of Bob Church's special size 12 short shank Mini Nobblers. In the flush of his triumph over the French, he re-christened them Frog Nobblers.

There are two basic versions: the yellow marabou and gold mylar model for which Bob gives the dressing here, and the white marabou and silver mylar version. John also has a Black Frog Nobbler with two turns of fluorescent chenille as a tag, and the rest of the body black chenille.

He uses a leader of 20–22 feet with a size 8 weight forward line, preferably with a back wind. Otherwise, he may shorten to 12 feet. At times, he will go down to a size 14 hook and overall length of almost 4 cms when fish are difficult on buzzers. The retrieve is radically different from the orthodox Frog Nobbler. John fishes the lure using a figure-of-eight retrieve. The Frog Nobbler is almost always taken quickly by the fish, and not followed first. If fish begin to follow and not take, then he changes over to one of the other colours. John believes that the success of the fly is engendered by the up and down motion, and it is essential to have a very large spray of marabou in the tail, and the two layers of lead wire to ensure this action.

How to tie

Hook:	Standard shank 10
Silk:	Yellow
Tail:	Yellow marabou, very generous
Underbody:	Two layers of lead wire along the length of the hook shank
Body:	Gold mylar

Run waxed silk from immediately behind the eye of the hook down the shank in neat, butting turns, and stop just before the bend is reached. The silk is then returned up the shank to the three quarter position ready to receive the rolled butt end of a shuttlecock plume of marabou.

Offer the butt end of the marabou plume up for tying in, and secure firmly on top of the shank at the three quarter position with firm turns of the tying silk travelling in the direction of the bend. Continue with the silk in firm, neat turns, lashing down the rolled butt as you go, and stop on reaching the end of the foundation laps of silk. Let the silk hang at anchor at this position whilst the lead underbody is applied.

Take a length of fine fly tyer's lead wire, and wind it in neat, touching turns from a position slightly in front of the anchored silk up the shank to within a short distance of the eye, and then back again to the anchored silk. The waste lead can now be cut away, and the raw end and the laps along the body secured. This can be done in two ways. The whole of the lead underbody can be given a soaking of Superglue and allowed to dry. Alternatively, it can be given a criss-crossed lashing with the tying silk which is started at the anchor position at the tail, taken over the lead in firm, open spirals, and then returned in the same manner back to the anchor position at the base of the marabou tail. Having secured the lead, we are now ready for the mylar body.

Mylar is not the easiest of materials to work with, particularly with hooks this small, because the cut ends will insist on becoming unwoven and splayed. It is for this reason I recommend that in this case you do not use a length of mylar the same size as the body which is the normal practice. Instead, I suggest that a much longer length is worked with, and only in the final stage is it actually cut to size. This is how it is done.

From the main hank of mylar, cut away a nice workable length of say 8 cms, and then pull out its string central core. Having done this, pinch the leading end together and cut a fresh end. This will get rid of the splayed ends for the time being. Now gently ease the mylar piping over the eye of the hook, along the lead underbody and up the start of the tail and the waiting, anchored silk. The piping can now be secured in this position with firm turns of the silk, and then finished off with a whip finish using an extra large loop which will pass over the rest of the body, mylar and all. On completing the whip finish, snip away the tying silk.

The next job is to pull the mylar piping tight so that it clings snugly to the lead underbody. The 6 or 7 cms extending beyond the eye of the hook will greatly assist in this. Having pulled the piping taut, the tying silk is then reintroduced over the top of the piping just behind the eye. The eye can easily be located by pressing the piping. Make several very firm turns of the silk to secure it, then take a pair of very fine pointed scissors, insert them just behind the eye through the mylar sheath, and snip away the excess by gradually working your way around the shank. The raw ends of the mylar can now be covered with firm turns of the silk, a neat head formed, and then whip finished. Two coats of cellire will complete the lure.

Geronimo

Brian Harris, its inventor, tells me that the Geronimo was tied for Grafham rainbows in the water's early years when they would chase and grab any very bright, mobile streamer-type lure near the surface in summer and clear water. He based it loosely on Taff Price's Orange Streamer and on the American Chief Needabeh streamer, which is why he thought up the name Geronimo! It did very well at Grafham and remains quite a popular pattern.

The Geronimo has a ruff of bright yellow and orange hackles which gives it an outline and movement similar to the Muddler, and it needs to be fished in the same way, that is on a floating line and long leader at a medium to fast pace designed to keep it either on or just below the surface, especially if there is a good ripple on the water.

David Collyer has given us a matuka version of this fly designed to avoid the occasional hangup of the wing around the bend. However, I prefer the streamer wing because it remains more mobile.

How to tie

Hook:	L/S 8–12
Silk:	Yellow
Tail:	Mixed, brown and yellow cock hackle fibres
Body:	Flat gold tinsel or lurex. If lurex is used, a ribbing of fine gold wire is essential
Wing:	Four well marked cree hackles
Hackles:	Rear, long-fibred orange cock: front, bright yellow cock

Run waxed silk from immediately behind the eye of the hook down the shank in neat, butting turns, and stop at a position opposite the point of the hook. Now, take a large brown and a large yellow cock hackle, and strip away from each a small bunch of fibres, taking care to keep their tips in line. The two bunches can then be placed together, carefully aligning their tips, and then gently rolled between finger and thumb in order to mix them together. The bunch of mixed fibres can now be offered up and tied in on top of the shank to form the tail of the lure, and the silk continued down the shank in neat, touching turns, lashing down the tail fibres as you go. Stop the silk just before the bend begins.

With your very first turn of the tying silk returning up the shank, catch in, if lurex is being used, a short length of fine gold wire, and then continue up the shank in neat, butting turns to within a short distance of the eye, allowing just enough room for the wing and two hackles. Now catch in a length of medium width flat gold tinsel or lurex with two or three firm turns of the silk. The tinsel can then be wound down the body in neat, touching turns until the start of the tail is reached, and then it is returned in the same manner back to the anchored tying silk where it is tied off with three firm turns of the silk and the waste cut away. If lurex is used, this is then followed by the gold wire which is wound over the gold body in firm, open and equally spaced spirals until the anchored silk is reached. On reaching the silk, tie the wire down and snip away the waste. The raw ends of the tinsel and wire can now be covered with neat turns of the tying silk which is then returned to the head end of the body ready to receive the wing.

For the wing, select four matching and well marked cree cock hackles, and place each pair tip on tip, one on top of the other. The two pairs of matched hackles can then themselves be paired up by placing them tip on tip, back to back (concave on concave). The four feathers are now gripped tightly in this position whilst the unwanted base flue and fibres are stripped away to expose the central stems, reducing the wing simultaneously to the required length.

The wing can now be offered up, and tied in by lashing the four exposed stems firmly on top of the hook shank. It is important that the commencement of the wing fibres is placed in line with the head end of the gold body. Having secured the hackle stems with four or five very firm turns of the silk, their waste ends can then be trimmed away at a shallow angle to the shank, and their ends covered with further firm turns of the silk. The silk can then be returned to the commencement of the wing fibres ready to receive the two hackles.

The first hackle to be tied in and wound on is a fairly long fibred dyed orange cock. Select a suitable hackle, strip away the base flue and any insignificant fibres, and then tie in close up to the start of the streamer wing with four or five firm turns of the silk travelling towards the eye. Now snip away the waste end of the hackle stem and attach the hackle pliers to the tip of the hackle. Four or five full turns of the hackle are now made around the shank of the hook, then it is tied off and the waste cut away. It is important that this first hackle has a nice backward rake. This is achieved by stroking the fibres backwards with the fingers and thumb of the left hand whilst several turns of the tying silk are taken over the roots.

The second hackle, a bright yellow cock slightly shorter in fibre than the first, can now be tied in nearest to the eye and wound on for four or five turns, one in front of the other, and then tied off and the waste cut away. This hackle should be allowed to stand slightly more proud than the last one, almost dry fly style but not quite, otherwise it will float like a dry fly, so take only one or two turns of the tying silk over the roots this time before forming a neat head with silk and the usual whip finish. Two coats of cellire will complete the lure.

Girdle Bug

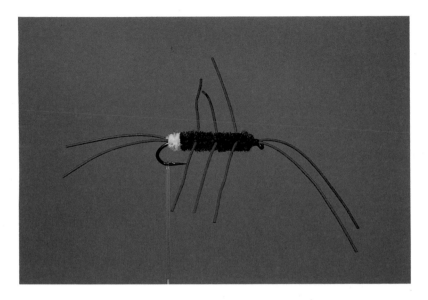

Many enterprising and original ideas in the realm of lures and fly dressing materials emanate from the United States and, although it is relatively new to this country, the Girdle Bug and similar dressings have been in use there for around thirty years. It was originally developed, Steve Parton tells me, from Popping and other Bass Bug dressings. The celebrated and progressive fly dresser, William Blades, was substantially responsible for the evolution of highly representative Western stonefly nymphs which incorporated lifelike rubber legs and antennae.

This pattern which has white legs for sunlight and black ones for cloudy conditions has been found to be startlingly effective on numerous waters in this country but, oddly enough, totally useless on others, and there is no obvious means of determining where the bug will work. So why not tie up a few, and have some fun trying them out on your own waters?

They are best fished slowly in foot pulls somewhat below the surface on floating or slow sinking lines. Their effectiveness has been found to be greater before the onset of fry feeding than after. Steve tells me that more exotic colour schemes have also been found to work. This can easily be achieved by changing the colour of the chenille body and the butt. I am sure you will have noticed, however, that the basic Girdle Bug body colours have distinct shades of the Viva!

How to tie

Hook:	L/S 2–12 (4X)
Silk:	Black
Butt:	DF Green chenille
Body:	Black chenille
Underbody:	Fine lead wire
Tails, legs & horns:	Black or white living rubber leg material

Run the waxed silk from a position approximately 3 mms behind the eye of the hook up the shank in neat, butting turns, and stop immediately behind the eye. Now take two 6 mm lengths of living rubber, match them up, and then tie them in side by side on top of the hook shank with the greater part of their length trailing over the eye of the hook. The silk is now wound down the shank in very firm, butting turns, tying down the short ends of the rubber as you go. It is a good idea to stretch the short ends during the lashing down process, because this not only reduces the bulkiness of the rubber but also makes a very secure job of things. On reaching the end of the 3 mm bed of foundation silk, trim the waste short ends of the rubber away while still drawing them tightly.

The silk is then continued down the shank, still using neat, butting turns, to a position 5 mms from the rear of the eye, the proportions being for a longshank size 6 4X. Now take a 7 mm length of living rubber, and lay it centrally across the top of the hook shank, that is horizontally and at 90 degrees. The rubber is then secured in this position with the tying silk using a figure of eight lashing. This done, the silk is continued on down the shank, again in butting turns, for another 5 mms whereupon another length of living rubber is tied in as before. Then, at a position 5 mms on, the third and final pair of legs is tied in to complete the set of three equally spaced pairs.

After the final pair of legs has been tied in, take two 5 mm lengths of living rubber which will be used to form the tails, pair them up so that their ends are in line, and then tie them in on top of the hook shank immediately behind the last set of legs. After catching the strands of rubber in by their tips, stretch them quite tightly as we did with the horns, and then continue with the silk down the shank, lashing down the rubber as you go. Stop the silk just before the bend begins.

With your very first turn of the tying silk returning up the shank, catch in a short length of DF green chenille by its stripped central core, and then take the silk forward 4 or 5 mms. The chenille is then wound forward in touching turns and, on reaching the anchored silk, tied off with three firm turns of the silk and the waste cut away. The completed butt should measure approximately 4 mms.

Now take a length of black chenille of approximately 10 to 12 cms, and tie it in close up to the butt by its stripped central core. The silk is then taken up the shank for 2 mms, and a 14 cm length of fine fly tyer's lead wire tied in before returning the silk back up the shank to a position 2 mms behind the eye.

The lead wire can now be wound up the shank in neat, touching turns, winding it carefully past the legs so as not to disturb their "set". On reaching the anchored silk, tie the lead wire off and cut away the waste. This is then followed by the black chenille, once again winding it in neat touching turns, and taking care to trap the legs in their final position, that is 90 degrees to the body. On reaching the anchored silk, tie the chenille off, cut away the waste, form a neat head with the tying silk, whip finish and then cut away the silk. The legs, tails and horns can now be trimmed to their desired length. On the sample sent to me by Steve Parton the dimensions are as follows: horns $4\frac{1}{2}$ cms, legs $2\frac{1}{2}$ cms and tails 3 cms. After the trimming, the head can be varnished in the usual manner.

Goldie

Yet another fine lure from Bob Church which, when fished deep with a lead-core head at the bottom of both the North and South Arms of Rutland Water, brought him and his friends many large browns. In a smaller 10 or 12 size it can be used as a tail fly fished loch style on a floating line in a team of three with Soldier Palmers or Grenadiers on the droppers. In this situation a fish will sometimes follow the Soldier Palmer and then be attracted by the bright gold body and yellow and black wing of the Goldie.

This lure provides a valuable colour alternative to the usual blacks, whites and oranges. A tandem version has been used successfully on a deep sink line in the blazing hot calm of high summer. Bob Church considers it a good all-round pattern, and has had days when it has out-fished any other fly. This includes days of high wind and big waves when a number 10 Goldie will take fish which are up but maybe not showing.

How to tie

Hook:	L/S 6–10
Silk:	Black
Tail:	Yellow cock hackle fibres
Body:	Flat gold tinsel or lurex
Rib:	Fine gold wire
Hackle:	Yellow cock hackle fibres, beard only
Underwing:	Yellow goat, skunk or squirrel hair
Overwing:	Black goat, skunk or squirrel hair
Head:	Black varnish

The tying sequence of the Goldie up to the point when the beard hackle is about to be added is identical to that already described for the Geronimo lure on page 78. Rather than unnecessarily repeating this let us pick up the tying at that stage.

First turn the hook over in the vice ready to receive the hackle, and make sure that the silk has been returned to the head end of the gold body. Next, select a large cock hackle which has been dyed bright yellow, and strip from it a fairly generous bunch of fibres, taking care to keep their tips in line. The bunch of fibres is then offered up and tied in to form a nice spray around the uppermost portion of the hook shank using firm, forward-travelling turns of the silk. After four or five turns, trim away the waste butts of the fibres, and then cover the cut ends with further firm turns of the silk which is then returned to the junction of the gold body and the start of the hackle. The hook can now be returned to its original position in the vice.

The underwing of yellow hair can now be prepared and tied in. The amount of hair required for the underwing of the Goldie is equivalent to slightly more than half the amount that would normally be used for a full wing, the remainder being made up by the overwing. To form the wing, select a bunch of hair as it lies on the skin in its natural position, and gently draw it into an upright position. As soon as the individual tips of the hairs come into line, tighten the grip on the bunch and crop it away at the roots. Next, comb out any underfur and any short or broken hairs which may be present at the base of the hairs. This done, the wing can be offered up and tied in.

As previously recommended in the tying descriptions for the Banded Squirrel Bucktail and the Church Fry, it is a good idea to bed the hair down into a small amount of fine cellire varnish. After tying the underwing in, cropping away the waste hair at a shallow angle and covering the raw butts with firm turns of the tying silk, the silk is then returned to the commencement of the underwing ready to receive the overwing of black hair.

The selection, preparation and tying in of the hair for the overwing is identical to that used for the underwing, only this time the amount of hair is slightly less. The main thing to aim for is that the base of the hackle, the end of the gold body and the lashings of silk which secure the wings are all in line with each other. Having tied in the overwing, cropped away the waste hair at a shallow angle and covered the butt ends with firm turns of the tying silk, all that remains is to form a neat head with the silk and whip finish. Two coats of cellire varnish will complete the lure.

Hairy Minnow

This minnow-like pattern was first introduced to anglers in 1972 in Taff Price's classic little *Lures for Game, Coarse and Sea Fishing* which I urge any serious lure fisherman to try to add to his fishing library if he can get hold of a copy. Taff says that when dry, the Hairy Bucktail Minnow, to give it its full name, looks like a sparse grotesque shaving brush, but, when wet it has a very lifelike appearance. One piece of advice he gives is not to overdress the fly.

Taff mentions that anglers have been successful with the Hairy Minnow at Chew and Blagdon, and I would certainly confirm this from personal experience at Chew where in the summer there are huge shoals of minnow and fry in the shallows which trout beat up with relish. Fished very slowly from the bank casting across the edges of the shoals, especially if there is a good chop on the water, can be very exciting. Brown trout taken in this way at Chew are some of the most beautiful fish to be caught anywhere.

How to tie

Hook:	L/S 8–10
Silk:	Black
Tail:	Small tuft of DFM red wool
Rib:	Oval silver
Body:	Flat silver
Wing:	Dark green bucktail, white bucktail underneath
Underwing or hackle:	White bucktail tied in to reach the bend of the hook, then a small tuft of red bucktail at the throat
Head:	Black, with white painted eye and black pupil

Run waxed silk from immediately behind the eye of the hook down the shank in neat, butting turns, and stop when one quarter of the shank has been covered. Now take a length of DFM red wool which is half as long again as the length of the hook, and tie it in on top of the shank by the tip. The silk is now continued down the shank in neat, very firm butting turns, lashing down the wool as you go. It is important that the wool is drawn tight during the tying down process, and kept in place on top of the shank. Stop the silk just before the bend begins. With your very first turn of the tying silk returning up the shank, catch in a length of fine number 14 oval silver tinsel, and then continue with the silk up the shank in neat, butting turns, lashing down the butt end of the oval tinsel as you go, and stop a short distance from the eye, allowing sufficient space for the hackle, wings and a fairly bold head.

A length of medium width number 3 flat silver tinsel can now be tied in at this point, and then wound down the shank in neat, touching turns until the tail is reached. On reaching the tail, the tinsel is then returned up the shank to the tying silk where it is tied off and the waste end cut away. Winding the tinsel down and then back over itself will give the best possible results, and is well worth that bit of extra effort. The body can now be ribbed.

Take hold of the oval tinsel as it hangs to the rear of the hook, and wind it over the tinsel body with firm, open and equally spaced turns. On reaching the anchored silk, tie the tinsel off and cut away the waste. The raw ends of the tinsels are now covered with firm turns of the silk which is then returned to the head end of the body ready to receive the hair hackle. The tail can now be drawn tight, cropped to length, and the individual fibres then flared out before turning the hook over in the vice ready to receive the hackle.

Now select a small bunch of white bucktail, or white goat which is a good substitute, and tie in to reach the bend of the hook. This is then followed by a shorter bunch of red bucktail which is laid over the white hair for approximately half its length. The waste ends of both bunches of hair are then trimmed away at a shallow angle to the shank, their butts given a drop of fine cellire varnish, and then bound firmly down with turns of silk travelling towards the eye. The silk can now be returned to the head end of the body, and the hook to its original position in the vice.

We are now ready for the wing which, like the hair hackle, consists of two separate bunches of hair, white underneath with dark green over. Select a suitable bunch of white hair, and tie in on top of the shank with firm turns of the silk travelling towards the eye. Only take the silk about halfway to the eye, and let it hang at anchor there whilst the green overwing is prepared. Having selected and prepared the overwing, offer it up, and tie in to lie neatly over the top of the white underwing. Lash the overwing firmly into position with turns of silk travelling back over those which were used to secure the white hair, and stop the silk when it comes into line with the whipping which secured the hackle at the head end of the body. The waste ends of the hair wing can now be trimmed away at a shallow angle to the shank, and their butt ends given a soaking of fine cellire varnish. Allow the varnish to disappear into the butt ends, and then bind them down with firm, forward travelling turns of the silk. Any varnish pressed out of the butts should be wiped away, and not allowed to foul the eye of the hook. Having secured the hair wing, a neat head can then be formed with the tying silk and whip finished.

The head can now be given two coats of cellire varnish, the second being applied after the first has had time to harden off. The eyes likewise are added later when the second coat of cellire is thoroughly hardened. For the best way of painting eyes see the instructions given for the Dog Nobbler Green Grizzly on page 65.

Haymaker

The subject of water colour and its effect on the colour of fly we fish is a fascinating one. Even pure water has a colour, which is blue, because it transmits blue light and absorbs the other colours of the rainbow. Few of our waters are like this. Ours are usually coloured by the presence of mud and peat and algae and daphnia. They are most commonly greenish in colour, and the contrast is greatest when the fly is red or orange. Such flies will be the most visible to the fish, though that does not guarantee that they will be taken.

Muddy, dirty water is often a yellowish-brown colour in which yellow light will be transmitted as long as it is not too thick. In these circumstances a yellow fly which reflects yellow light will be the most visible. This is when to use lures like Yellow Fellow and Mrs Palmer. And, of course, David Collyer's Haymaker. David first used it when fishing with a farmer friend at Bough Beech Reservoir after weeks of rain and in algae thick water. He took a bag limit, but only after his farmer friend had left him in the warm sunshine for haymaking. So he decided to call the new fly Haymaker. David tells me that he still considers it one of his best flies, especially in murky conditions.

Try the Haymaker generally pulled smartly through the water just under the surface, and watch out for the furrow of a following rainbow.

How to tie

Hook:	L/S 6–10
Silk:	Black or yellow
Tail:	Bright yellow marabou
Body:	Yellow chenille
Underwing:	Yellow marabou
Overwing:	Yellow bucktail
Head:	Yellow varnish
Eyes:	Red varnish with black centre

Run the waxed silk from immediately behind the eye of the hook down the shank in neat, butting turns, and stop at a position opposite the point. Now take a small plume of yellow marabou fibres, and tie them in on top of the shank to form the tail of the lure. The overall length of the tail for a longshank size 6 should be approximately $1\frac{1}{2}$ to 2 cms. The silk is now continued down the shank, again in neat, butting turns, tying down the tail as you go. Stop the silk just before the bend begins.

With your very first turn of the tying silk returning up the shank, catch in a length of yellow chenille by its stripped central core after which the silk is returned up the shank in neat, touching turns, tying down the butt end of the chenille as you go. Stop the silk 3 or 4 mms, depending on the hook size, behind the eye. The chenille can now be wound up the shank in neat, touching turns and, on reaching the anchored silk, tied off with three firm turns of the silk and the waste chenille then cut away. After covering the raw butt of the chenille with firm turns of the tying silk, it is then returned to the head end of the chenille body ready to receive the underwing.

For the wing, select a fairly generous bunch of yellow marabou fibres, and spin them into the shuttlecock formation as described for the tying of the Cat's Whisker on page 50. Having prepared the marabou, it can then be offered up, and tied in on top of the hook shank by its spun, tapered butt. The tips of the wing should be positioned so as to come level with the tips of the tail. Secure the wing with four or five very firm, forward travelling turns of the tying silk before trimming away the waste butts at a shallow angle to the shank. The raw butts are then covered with further firm turns of the tying silk which is then returned to the commencement of the marabou wing ready to receive the overwing.

A bunch of yellow bucktail is now selected, trying to keep the tips in line, and then offered up and tied in immediately over the top of the marabou underwing. Once again, align the tips of the marabou and the hair before securing them into position with very firm, forward travelling turns of the silk. After four or five turns of the silk, trim away the waste butts of the bucktail, again at a shallow angle to the shank, and then cover their raw ends with further firm turns. A neat head can now be formed with the tying silk which is then whip finished and the waste cut away.

All that now remains to complete the lure is to give the head two coats of yellow cellire varnish, and then, when perfectly hardened off, the eye detail can be added.

Jack Frost

The effectiveness of marabou as a winging material was first demonstrated to the angling public by Bob Church's Appetiser. In 1974, he followed up this success with an equally killing lure, Jack Frost. The responsiveness of the marabou to the slightest movement, the translucency of the polythene body over the white fluorescent wool, and the dash of crimson in the hackle and tail make it a wonderful fry imitator in the latter part of the season.

Fished very slowly, it seems to work on most waters. Sometimes flies work for you in ways which are difficult to explain. There are times, at Hanningfield for instance later in the season, when the hatch of midges towards evening produces rises which do not respond to the usual chironomid imitations. Cast quickly into the ring of a rise or the path of a trout, I find a Jack Frost will sometimes be snapped up almost as soon as it lands by previously dour and finicky fish. Whether or not this dramatically disturbs the trout's feeding preoccupation I do not know, but it has rescued me from frustrated despair on more than one occasion when boat fishing.

How to tie

Hook:	L/S 6–10
Silk:	White
Tail:	Crimson wool
Body:	White fluorescent wool covered by a one eighth wide strip of polythene
Wing:	Generous spray of white marabou
Hackles:	Long-fibred crimson cock followed by long-fibred white cock

Run the waxed silk from immediately behind the eye of the hook down the shank in neat, butting turns, and stop when one quarter of the shank has been covered. Now take a length of crimson wool which is half as long again as the length of the hook, and tie in on top of the shank by its tip. The silk is now continued down the shank in neat, very firm, butting turns, lashing down the wool as you go. It is important that the wool is drawn tight during the tying down process, and kept in place on top of the shank. Stop the silk just before the bend begins. With your very first turn of the tying silk returning up the shank catch in a length of white fluorescent wool, and then continue with the silk up the shank, lashing down the butt end of the wool as you go, and stop a short distance from the eye allowing sufficient space for the wing and hackle. The crimson wool can now be cropped to length and flared out as explained for the Christmas Tree on page 56.

The white wool can now be wound up the shank in neat, butting turns until the tying silk is reached. On reaching the silk, tie the wool off with three firm turns of the silk, and cut away the waste wool. The raw ends of the wool can now be covered with firm turns of the tying silk, and then returned to the head end of the body. Now take the length of polythene strip, and tie in at the head of the body. This done, the polythene is then wound down the wool body in neat, touching turns until the tail is reached, and then returned back up the shank in the same manner to the tying silk. On reaching the silk, tie the polythene off and cut away the waste. The raw end of the polythene is now covered with firm turns of the silk, and then returned to the head end of the body ready to receive the wing.

For the wing, we will require a generous spray of marabou fibres which have been spun into the shuttlecock formation described earlier for the Cat's Whisker on page 50. Having prepared the wing, it is then tied in on top of the shank close up to the body with several firm turns of the silk. The spun butts of the plume are then cropped

93

away at a shallow angle to the shank, and their raw ends covered with firm turns of the silk. The silk can then be returned to the commencement of the wing ready to receive the hackles.

For the hackles, select a crimson and a white cock hackle, both of which should be long in the fibre. After stripping away the base flue from both of the hackles, offer the crimson one up and tie in close up to the wing. Now make two full turns of the hackle around the shank, and then tie off and cut away the waste. The white hackle can now be offered up, and tied in close up to the last turn of the crimson hackle, and then wound on for three full turns. The hackle can then be tied off and the waste cut away.

In his book, *Reservoir Trout Fishing*, Bob Church emphasised that the hackles of the Jack Frost should be tied down so that they sweep back towards the tail. This is how it is done. Encompass the whole ruff of hackles with the fingers and thumb of the left hand, and draw them backwards whilst at the same time covering their roots with touching turns of the tying silk. Release the hackles from time to time to see how they are responding to this treatment, then, when sufficient rake has been achieved, form a neat head with the tying silk and whip finish. Two coats of white cellire varnish will complete the lure.

Jersey Herd

The most common form of advertising is the claim that some product is "new" and therefore, by implication, better. This is nowhere more true than in the realm of flies which are constantly being invented and reinvented. The Jersey Herd is a first-generation lure produced by Tom Ivens as early as 1951. It may not be as commonly seen in fly boxes as it was, but, of course, is still just as effective.

It was designed in either its weighted or unweighted form to be heavy enough to stay submerged despite a fast recovery. Tom's rush-tied job that Whitsuntide took him bag limits on three successive days, and because he used the only "gold" tinsel available to him, namely the foil from the top of a bottle of Channel Island milk, he gave it the splendidly imaginative name of Jersey Herd.

The inventor described it as a minnowish creation, but it is worth noticing that here again is a fly with a rich orange in it, in this case, the hackle. I recollect my old fishing partner, Alan Meakin, pulling in a limit bag of rainbows on my own lake many years ago whilst I struggled for one. His secret? A "new" fly: a Jersey Herd!

Bob regards the Jersey Herd with great affection because it was the first lure he ever used way back in 1963 at Eye Brook Reservoir. Its success made it a firm favourite of his, but even before he began to tie his own flies, he had firm ideas about the dressing. The flow of the peacock herl which formed the tail and back had to lie in the right direction, namely from head to tail, the body had to be nicely tapered and the head to be fairly large and distinct.

Though it will take its share of fish throughout, Bob feels that the warm-water period of high summer through to September is its peak killing time, fished on the point position with a floating line, to produce that exciting furrow of a following trout. An excellent variation on the original is a slim, gold body and lemon/yellow hackle.

How to tie

Hook:	L/S 6–10
Silk:	Black
Tail & back:	Eight to twelve strands of bronze peacock herl
Body:	Medium to wide copper coloured, flat tinsel or lurex over a shaped, floss silk underbody
Rib:	Optional, but if lurex is to be used to form the body, then it is essential that a rib of fine copper wire be added
Hackle:	Dyed rich orange cock hackle, fairly short in fibre, two or three full turns
Head:	Three or four strands of peacock herl, twisted into a rope and wound on, or, alternatively, as described in the tying instructions

The method of tying the Jersey Herd which I am about to give is one that I have been using for the past twenty odd years, and it does differ slightly from that given by its inventor, Tom Ivens, in his pioneer book, *Still Water Fly-Fishing.* The important thing is that the end result is exactly the same.

Run waxed silk from directly behind the eye of the hook down the shank in neat, butting turns, and stop just before the bend begins. Now select eight to twelve peacock herls, and lay them all facing in the same direction. The amount used will be dependent on the quality of the herls and the density of the flue. The bunch of herls can now be offered up for tying in on top of the hook shank. It is important that the flow of the herl fibres (flue) runs from head to tail of the lure, and that there is a generous overhang of herls both at the bend of the hook and at the eye. Having offered the herls up thus, they can then be secured with several very firm turns of the silk travelling in the direction of the eye. Having secured the herls on top of the hook shank, the forward facing herls are then lifted and laid back over the tail out of the way whilst the body is formed.

If a ribbing is to be added, it is at this point that it is tied in. Take a length of copper wire, and catch it in by bringing the tying silk, which is still hanging at anchor after tying the herl in at the start of the bend, over the shank immediately in front of the laid back herl, and secure it with three or four firm turns. This is then followed by the tying in of a length of copper coloured tinsel or lurex. Make sure that both the wire and the tinsel are secured close up to the whippings of tying silk which have secured the herls to the shank. The silk can now be returned up the shank in neat, butting turns, lashing down the raw ends of the wire and tinsel as you go, and stop at a point a short distance from the eye, allowing just enough space for the hackle and the head.

A length of silk floss or fine wool can now be tied in at this position, and then wound down the shank to the junction of the tail and back herls, and then back up the shank again. This winding is repeated several more times, each time shortening the distance covered by the floss, until a fish-shaped underbody is formed. On returning to the anchored tying silk for the last time, the floss is tied off and the waste cut away.

The copper tinsel or lurex is now wound neatly over the floss underbody and, on reaching the anchored tying silk, tied off and the waste cut away. This is then followed by the copper wire which is wound in firm, open and equally spaced turns until the silk is reached, whereupon the wire is tied off and the waste cut away. The raw ends of the tinsel and copper wire can now be covered with firm turns of the silk which is then returned to the head end of the body ready to receive the back material.

Take hold of the herls which have been laid out of the way over the tail, and position them neatly over the back of the lure, securing in place with several firm turns of the silk. The waste ends of the herls can then be cut away, and their butts covered with firm turns of the silk which is then returned to the head end of the body and back material ready to receive the hackle. For the hackle, select a short-fibred, orange-dyed cock hackle, and tie it in by its stripped stem close up to the body. Make two or three full turns of the hackle around the shank, and then tie it off and snip away the waste. The hackle fibres are now stroked backwards with the fingers and thumb of the left hand whilst the roots of the fibres are covered with three turns of the silk to give just a slight backwards slant. All that remains now is the head.

My method of forming the head is to use a single strand of peacock herl to form the characteristic bold head of the Jersey Herd. The herl should be chosen from just below the eye of the peacock feather. This is where the herls with the heaviest flue are found, and it is important that the herl is tied in close up to the hackle with the quill of strand leading (facing the eye) and the flue trailing. The silk is then returned to a position just behind the eye ready to receive and tie down the herl after the herl is completed. Now take hold of the strand of herl, and wind it forward to the eye in very close turns, making sure that it is the quill edge that is leading. Done correctly, it will throw up a very bushy and bold head. On reaching the tying silk tie the herl off, snip away the waste, and then whip finish. The tail can now be trimmed to length. The length of the finished tail should be between 8 and 12 mms depending on the hook size. To achieve this neatly, simply take hold of the herls as they trail behind the bend, pull them tightly in line with the shank, and make one crisp, measured cut. All that remains to be done is to place a drop of fine cellire varnish on the whippings at the head and the junction of the tail.

The Leaded DF Doll

Another Richard Walker modification of the Baby Doll. He discarded the back because, as it was the same white colour as the body, he could not see what useful purpose it served. However, the main difference in design from the original is the incorporation of lead foil lengthwise along the top of the hook shank to make it sink faster and lie with the hook point upwards, thus avoiding snags when fished on or near the bottom. The crimson or orange-dyed cock hackle fibres tied in above the body act as a beard or false hackle when it is in the water in its reversed posture.

The Leaded DF Doll's sinking quality is invaluable for searching various depths of water, and in dark or churned up water it is splendidly visible.

How to tie

Hook:	L/S 6–8
Silk:	White
Tail:	DF white wool

Body:	DF white wool
Underbody:	Three layers of thin lead foil lengthwise along the top of the hook shank
False hackle:	Crimson or orange-dyed cock hackle fibres tied in above the body

Having already tied or seen the tying of the Baby Doll, Nell Gwynne and the Undertaker, it will immediately be realised that the Leaded DF Doil is a dressing which is performed on very similar lines. The main differences are the abolition of the wool back material, the addition of a beard or false hackle and an underbody of fine lead foil.

The first job when tying the Leaded DF Doll is to run waxed silk from behind the eye of the hook, down the shank in neat, butting turns to stop at a point midway between the point of the hook and the commencement of the bend. It is at this point that a slim strip of lead foil (obtained from the neck caps of good quality wines) is bound down along the top of the shank to within a short distance of the eye. A slightly shorter strip of foil is now lashed in place on top of the last after being centralised, and the silk then taken down the shank in neat, butting turns. The third and final strip of foil – which is once again slightly shorter than its predecessor – is positioned centrally and lashed firmly into place with neat, butting turns of the tying silk returning up the shank.

The silk is now wound down the shank to a position immediately before the bend begins and there left to hang at anchor while the tail is prepared. For the tail, cut two or three (depending on thickness) short lengths of white DF wool – they need not be too long, about 38 mm is sufficient – and lay them side by side with their forward facing tips in line with each other. Now take the three pieces of wool and tie them in as one by their tips on top of the hook shank immediately above the anchored silk. Lash the butt ends of wool down with neat, butting turns as you return the silk up the shank to within a short distance of the eye of the hook, leaving the excess tail material to trail behind the bend. This will be trimmed to length later.

A fresh length of white DF wool can now be tied in just behind the eye, and then wound down the shank to the tail and back again, forming a fish-shaped body by tightening up or flattening out the turns of wool as you go. On returning to the anchored silk, tie off the wool and cut away the waste. It is at this point that the wool body is given a rubbing all over with fine glasspaper to fluff up the wool and give it a velvety texture which emphasises the fluorescent qualities. Now crop the tail to length and flare out the individual fibres.

All that remains now to complete the tying is to add a beard or false hackle of dyed hot-orange or crimson cock hackle fibres to the top of the shank, form a neat head with the tying silk and then whip finish. Two applications of cellire varnish, the second after the first one is completely dry, will give a deep, heavy gloss finish to the head.

The Leadhead

Richard Walker had one of the most fertile and precise minds in British angling, and it was he who first introduced the idea of a pinched lead shot behind the eye of the hook following the study of American patterns. This he incorporated into the Leadhead, the precursor of the Dog Nobbler. Why the latter developed into so much more of a killer was in the addition of the long marabou tail.

The Leadhead, however, has its own uses insomuch as it can be fished deep on a floating line, retrieved at a modest pace, yet rarely catch weed or snags as it fishes hook point upwards. If you want to make the most of the up and down motion engendered by the split shot, then you must retrieve it in short jerks like the Dog Nobbler. As Bob mentions in the dressing, it can be tied in a variety of colour combinations.

How to tie

Hook: L/S R/B 8–10 forged or flattened
Head: BB shot or smaller, just behind the eye

Body:	Floss or wool ribbed with oval tinsel
Wing:	A bunch of suitable hair
Useful colours:	Yellow wing, light brown head, arc Chrome DF wool or floss body, ribbed oval silver
	Natural grey squirrel wing, brown head, red DF wool body
	Black wing, black head, red DF wool body

The construction of the Leadhead begins in much the same way as did the Dog Nobblers, described earlier in the book, with the fixing of a BB shot or smaller to the shank just behind the eye of the hook. In the case of the Leadhead, however, the shot is set back 2 or 3 mms from the eye, and the painted eyes are not added until the lure is completed.

So, having fixed the shot to the hook shank, the tying can begin. Run waxed silk from directly behind the lead shot down the shank in neat, butting turns, and stop at a point just before the bend begins. With your very first turn of the tying silk returning up the shank, catch in a length of fine oval silver tinsel and, with your second turn, a length of wool. The silk is then returned up the shank in neat, butting turns, lashing the butt ends of the tinsel and wool as you go, to stop close up to the lead shot.

The wool can now be wound up the shank in neat, butting turns and, on reaching the anchored silk, tied down with three firm turns of the silk. The waste wool is then cut away. Now take hold of the tinsel and rib the wool body with firm, open spirals. On reaching the silk, tie the tinsel down and cut away the waste. The raw ends of the wool and tinsel can now be covered with firm turns of the tying silk, and we are ready for the hair wing.

Select a suitable bunch of hair, offer it up, and tie in close up to the lead shot. After cutting away the waste ends of the hair, soak their butts with an application of vycoat, and then bind them down very firmly indeed. Continue with the whippings of silk and the occasional application of vycoat until the silk builds up, and merges smoothly with the lead shot. As soon as this happens, whip finish and cut away the silk. The silk can now be reintroduced to the shank just behind the eye, and the same sort of tapered bindings built up again. After whip finishing and cutting away the silk, the whole head which includes the whippings on both sides of the lead shot and the lead shot itself, can be given a coat of vycoat and then set aside to thoroughly harden off.

Once the head is dry, it can be painted the appropriate colour using either Humbrol enamel or a plastic paint, and then set aside again to dry. After the paint has completely dried, the eyes can be added. This is done in exactly the same way as was described for the Dog Nobbler Green Grizzly on page 65. Then, after the eyes have dried, the lure is completed by giving the whole head a coat of polyurethane varnish.

Leprechaun

I tend to regard this as one of those occasional lures which, on its day, can be a real killer. The Leprechaun was introduced by Peter Wood in 1972, and has a green wing and tail, and fluorescent lime-green chenille for the body. Its colour makes it a very distinctive lure belonging to that group which works best in midsummer when there is a lot of algae about, and rainbows respond to something gaudy and fished fast on the big reservoirs. It can also be a deadly lure fished rather more slowly if you have located shoals of rainbows mopping up daphnia 10 to 15 feet down. In a smaller size and leaded, I have seen it take some big fish used as a stalking fly on smaller waters like Rockbourne Trout Fishery and Rooksbury Mill.

How to tie

Hook:	L/S 6–10
Silk:	Black
Tail:	Dyed green cock hackle fibres
Rib:	Flat silver tinsel

Body:	Fluorescent lime-green chenille
Wing:	Four matched green cock hackles
Throat hackle:	Green cock hackle fibres

The method and sequence for the tying of the Leprechaun is identical to that already described for the Black Chenille, and it is only the colour of the materials that is different. So, in order to avoid unnecessary repetition, please refer to the Black Chenille for tying instructions on page 29.

Marabou Tadpole

Tadpoles are a familiar sight in the early months of the season on many waters ranging from the smallest to the largest. Attempts to imitate them have evolved into an exceptionally deadly lure for reservoir trout. The original models have undergone considerable modifications from innovative anglers to cater for their ever changing seasonal needs and the moods of the trout.

The basic black tadpole now appears in a range of colours of which the favourites are yellow, orange, red and green. Quite often DF chenilles and dyed DF marabou plumes are used to make the lure more visible in water with reduced light penetration due to daphnia or algal blooms, or, indeed, wave action.

You can then choose whether or not to have a lead underbody. Bob reminds us that the addition of lead not only influences the depth at which the lure may be fished but also its action in the water. An unleaded Tadpole will tend to "swim" on a level plane like any other conventional lure. However, as soon as a lead underbody is added, the action becomes very similar to that of a Dog Nobbler albeit less pronounced.

Strange as it may seem, some days one particular action will appeal more to trout than the other. So it is wise to carry a few of both versions with you just to be on the safe side.

How to tie

Hook:	8–10
Silk:	Black
Tail:	A plume of black marabou or any other desired colour
Body:	Black chenille tied a fat tadpole shape or other appropriate colour
Underbody:	Optional, fine lead wire

Run waxed silk from immediately behind the eye of the hook down the shank in neat, butting turns, and stop just before the bend begins. The silk is now returned back up the shank, this time in open spirals, to stop approximately 3 mms from the eye. What we have just formed is a non-slip foundation on which to secure the marabou plume which will form the tail of the lure. Marabou is a very slippery material, and must never be tied directly to a bare hook shank.

Next, prepare a fairly generous plume of black marabou fibres, and tie in on top of the shank at the position at which the silk is now anchored. Continue with the silk down the shank in neat, butting turns, lashing down the marabou as you go, and stop when the last lap of the foundation bed of silk is reached. If this is to be a leaded Tadpole, then it is at this point that the lead is added.

Take a length of fine, fly tyer's lead, and commence to wind it along the shank in neat, butting turns from a position approximately 2 mms up from the start of the tail, to end at a point about 2 to 3 mms behind the eye. After winding the lead firmly along the shank, trim away the waste ends and secure the lead in place by taking firm, open spirals of the tying silk over the laps of lead for its entire length, and then back again in the same manner to the starting point. Done correctly, this will form a criss-crossed pattern with the laps of tying silk which will lock the lead firmly in place. The silk should now be positioned close up to the start of the tail ready to receive the chenille which will form the body of the lure.

Now take an 8 to 10 mm length of fine, black chenille, and catch it in with the silk by its stripped central core. Continue with the silk up the shank, lashing down the butt end of the chenille core as you go, and over the lead underbody to stop at a position just behind the eye. The body can now be formed by winding the chenille up to the tying silk. This can be done in one go or, as I prefer to do it, in three goes, thereby forming a nice tapered effect. To create the tapered effect, first wind the chenille up to the silk, then back down the shank almost to the starting point, but not quite, and then back again to the anchored tying silk, whereupon the chenille is tied down and the waste end cut away. All that remains to complete the lure is to form a neat head with the tying silk, whip finish and varnish.

Mickey Finn

When a top lure expert like Bob Church tells us that of the five attractors he tied for his book, *Reservoir Trout Fishing*, one was the Mickey Finn, and we also know that for many years it has been a top American pattern, then we have to seriously consider having it in our fly box.

Although the bucktail wings are yellow and red, the overall effect firmly places the Mickey Finn in the orange group of lures such as the Whisky, Chief Needabeh and Church Fry. It works best, therefore, in high water temperatures and plenty of algae, retrieved in the top few feet of water at fast or very fast speeds to attract aggressive rainbows.

How to tie

Hook:	L/S 6–12
Silk:	Black
Rib:	Oval silver tinsel
Body:	Flat silver tinsel
Wing:	Small bunch of yellow bucktail, then red in the

middle and yellow bucktail on top. For the smallest of the hook sizes dyed squirrel is a better proposition

Throat hackle: Dyed red cock hackle, optional

Run waxed silk from immediately behind the eye of the hook down the shank in neat, butting turns, and stop just before the bend begins. With your very first turn of the tying silk returning up the shank, catch in a 10 cm length of fine oval tinsel, and then continue up the shank in neat, butting turns, tying down the butt end of the tinsel as you go, and stop a short distance from the eye, allowing just enough space for the hackle and the hair wing.

Now catch in at this point a length of medium width flat silver tinsel, or, if you prefer it, lurex, with two or three firm turns of the silk. The tinsel can then be wound down the shank in neat, butting turns until the last lap of the foundation turns is reached. Having got there, the tinsel is then returned back up the shank, again in neat, touching turns, and, on reaching the anchored silk, tied down and the waste cut away. This is then followed by the oval silver tinsel which is wound over the silver body in firm, open and equally spaced spirals until the anchored silk is reached. At this point, tie the oval tinsel down and snip away the waste. The raw ends of the flat and oval tinsel can now be covered with neat turns of the tying silk travelling in the direction of the eye. This done, the silk is then returned to the head end of the body ready to receive the beard or false hackle.

First, turn the hook over in the vice. Now select a large red-dyed cock hackle, and strip away from it a fairly generous bunch of fibres, taking care to keep their tips in line. The bunch of fibres is then offered up and tied in to form a nice spray around the uppermost portion of the hook shank using firm, forward travelling turns of silk. After four or five turns, trim away the waste butts of the hackle fibres, and then cover their cut ends with further firm turns of the silk. The silk can then be returned to the junction of the silver body and the start of the hackle, and the hook to its original position in the vice.

We are now ready for the hair wing which in this case is comprised of three distinct bunches of hair, each one being tied in separately. I will describe how to select, prepare and tie in the first of the three bunches, and the other two can then be dealt with in a similar manner. First, select a suitable bunch of hair as it lies on the tail in its natural position. Take hold of the hair, and draw it into an upright position, keeping a close watch on the tips of the individual hairs.

As soon as they come into line, tighten your grip on the bunch, and crop it away from the tail close to the roots. The next job is to comb out any underfur and any short or broken hairs. This done, the bunch can be measured up, and tied in on top of the shank with four or five very firm, forward travelling turns of the silk before cropping away the waste ends of the hair at a shallow angle to the shank.

The second, red, bunch is now offered up and positioned over the top of the first, taking care to align their tips, and then secured firmly into position with very firm turns of the silk travelling back over the top of those which secured the first bunch. Stop when the silk comes into line with the turns of silk which first secured the underwing. The waste ends of the second bunch of hair can now be trimmed away, again at a shallow angle to the shank.

The third and final bunch of yellow hair is now offered up and tied in, this time with forward travelling turns of silk, and the waste ends trimmed away at the usual angle. The raw butts of hair can now be given a drop of fine cellire varnish, and then lashed firmly down. All that remains now is to form a neat head with the tying silk and whip finish. Two coats of cellire varnish will complete the lure.

Minnow Streamer

The criticism of lure fishing from the more purist minded anglers is that the lure is a piece of ironmongery that imitates nothing in particular. Interestingly, it is quite remarkable how many lures are representations of small fish, tadpole or even leech. About half the lures in this book are deceivers.

Almost twenty years ago, Conrad Voss Bark wrote an article about a fly used by his grandfather at Blagdon to simulate a minnow. Taff Price's Minnow Streamer is in a similar vein and, for the purists, he even gives us both a male and a female version, though he points out that both are equally successful.

John Wadham mentioned to me recently that his Poodle fly seemed to have lost its effect at Rutland where the fish regard anything with marabou as "dangerous". It is probably coincidence or personal preference, but certainly in the current season I have had much more success with streamer flies than with marabou on fisheries large and small. Black Ghost set the pace early in the season, and in warmer weather in June Minnow Streamer came into its own. One red-hot day at Croxley Hall Waters when fishing was extremely difficult, it was my only successful fly. There were shoals of minnow in the water, and a slow to medium retrieve keeping the fly a few inches below the surface did the trick.

How to tie

Hook:	L/S 6–10
Silk:	Olive
Tail:	Blue dun hackles
Rib:	Oval silver tinsel
Body:	White floss or wool. The new Datam glo-brite fluorescent floss makes a very attractive body for this lure
Wing:	Olive cock hackle feathers, back to back
Cheek:	Barred teal or mallard
Hackle:	Red beard hackle. Blue dun for the female minnow
Eye:	Two jungle cock or substitute tied short, or painted eye
Head:	Painted olive on top and white beneath

Run waxed silk from immediately behind the eye of the hook down the shank in neat, butting turns, and stop opposite the point of the hook. Now take a large cock hackle dyed blue dun, and strip from it a small bunch of fibres, taking care to keep their tips in line. The bunch of fibres can now be offered up, and tied in on top of the shank. Whilst holding the tail fibres in position, continue with the silk in neat, butting turns to a point just before the bend begins.

With your very first turn of the tying silk returning up the shank, catch in about 8 cms of fine oval silver tinsel, and then continue up the shank in neat, butting turns, stopping approximately 4 mms from the back of the eye. The white wool or floss can now be tied in at this point. If wool is to be used, then split it down, and use just one ply in order to avoid unnecessary bulk in the body. The length of the body material will vary from one to another depending on its individual thickness. However, 12 to 14 cms will usually be ample. Having tied in the wool or floss with three or four firm turns of the tying silk, it can then be wound down the shank to the commencement of the tail fibres, and then back to the tying silk where it is tied off with three firm turns of the silk. The waste body material can then be snipped away. Now take hold of the oval tinsel, and rib the body with six or seven firm, open spirals until the anchored silk is reached. At this point tie the tinsel off with three firm turns of the tying silk, and then cut away the waste tinsel. The raw ends of the body material and tinsel can now be covered with firm, forward

114

travelling turns of the tying silk, and then it is returned to the head end of the body.

Now turn the hook over in the vice ready to receive the hackle. Select a large cock hackle, either dyed-scarlet or blue dun, depending on which version you happen to be tying, and strip away from it a fairly generous bunch of fibres, taking care to keep their tips in line. Having prepared the fibres, offer them up and tie in to form a nice spray around the uppermost portion of the hook shank. Having done this, cut away the waste ends of the fibres, and cover their butts with firm turns of the tying silk. The hook can now be returned to its original position in the vice, and the silk to the head end of the body ready to receive the wing.

For the wing, select two or four olive-dyed cock hackles. I prefer four feathers in my streamer style lures. In my opinion this creates a better silhouette and a more substantial lure. Having selected your feathers, place each pair tip on tip, one on top of the other. The two pairs of matched hackles can then themselves be paired up by placing them tip on tip, back to back (concave on concave). The four feathers are now gripped tightly in this position whilst the unwanted base flue and fibres are stripped away to expose the central stems, at the same time reducing the wing to the required length.

The wing can now be offered up, and tied in by lashing the four exposed stems firmly on top of the hook shank. It is important that the commencement of the wing fibres is positioned in line with the head end of the body and the start of the hackle. Having secured the hackle stems with four or five very firm turns of the silk, their waste ends can then be trimmed away at a shallow angle to the shank, and their ends covered with further firm turns of the silk. The silk can now be returned to the commencement of the wing fibres ready to receive the cheeks.

For the cheeks, select two small, matching and well marked teal or mallard body feathers, and prepare by stripping away all the base flue and any superfluous fibres. The overall length of prepared cheek feathers should be fractionally longer than the body of the lure plus the exposed stems. Having prepared the cheek feathers, offer them up and tie in by positioning one on either side of the streamer wing, after which the waste ends of the cheek feather stems can be trimmed away, a neat head formed with the tying silk, and then finished off with the usual whip finish. All that now remains to complete this very attractive lure is to paint the head and eyes.

Missionary

This is a lure with a distinctive action in the water that sets it apart from almost any other fly. Dick Shrive's version, which is the one universally used, employs a whole grey mallard feather or a teal breast feather for the wing which is set low over the body and vibrates as the fly sinks. This is when the fish often take.

Trout will often attack a shoal of fry or minnow, leaving a number wounded. They may return to pick up these stragglers. The Missionary, slowly sinking with a slight to-and-fro motion caused by the flat wing, perfectly simulates the wounded little fish.

When trout are feeding on daphnia they are often susceptible to lures, but the problem arises of locating their depth which depends on the intensity of the light. Bob Church uses a Missionary for what he calls the countdown style of fishing. The idea is to cast out the lure on a floater or sink tip, and to count as it sinks slowly down in the water. Rainbows will often take the Missionary on the drop and, in so doing, leave you with a pretty accurate estimate of the depth of the daphnia layer.

How to tie

Hook: L/S 6–8
Silk: Black
Tail: Dark ginger or red cock hackle fibres. Crimson or scarlet
            cock hackle fibres are also commonly used
Rib: Flat silver tinsel
Body: White chenille, fluorescent for preference
Wing: Whole grey mallard or teal breast feather, set flat, one and
            a half times the hook's length
Hackle: Dark ginger or red cock hackle fibres, tied false. Crimson
            or scarlet cock hackle fibres are also commonly used

Run waxed silk from immediately behind the eye of the hook down the shank in neat, butting turns, and stop opposite the point of the hook. Now, take a large cock hackle feather – the choice of colours is given above – and strip away from it a small bunch of fibres, taking care to keep their tips in line. The bunch of fibres can now be offered up, and tied in on top of the shank. Whilst holding the tail fibres in position, continue with the silk in neat, butting turns to a point just before the bend begins.

With your very first turn of the tying silk returning up the shank, catch in about 8 cms of flat silver tinsel. Do not use lurex type tinsels for ribbing purposes as they will not stand up to the trout's teeth. With your second turn of tying silk returning up the shank, catch in a 10 cm length of white chenille by its stripped central core. The silk is then continued up the shank in neat, butting turns, tying down the ends of the tinsel and chenille core as you go. Stop the silk at a position short of the eye, allowing just enough space to accommodate the hackle and the wing. The chenille body can now be formed.

Take hold of the chenille by its tip, and wind it up the shank in neat, butting turns. On reaching the anchored silk, tie the chenille off with three or four firm turns of the silk and cut away the waste. This is then followed by the tinsel which is wound in firm, open spirals over the chenille. On reaching the silk, tie the tinsel off with three or four firm turns and then cut away the waste. The raw ends of the chenille and tinsel can now be covered with firm, forward travelling turns of the tying silk which is then returned to the head end of the body ready to receive the beard hackle.

First, turn the hook over in the vice ready to receive the hackle. Now select a large cock hackle in your chosen colours, and strip away from it a fairly generous bunch of fibres, taking care to keep their tips in line. Having prepared the fibres, now offer them up and tie in to form a nice spray around the uppermost portion of the hook shank. Having done this, cut away the waste ends of the fibres, and cover their butts with firm turns of the tying silk. The hook can now be returned to its original position in the vice and the silk returned to the head end of the body ready to receive the wing.

The wing for the modern day version of the Missionary is quite unique, but tends to be a bit of a stumbling block for many beginners to fly tying. What we are aiming for is a wing that is approximately one and a half times the length of the hook which, at the same time, is spoon shaped in all aspects, so selection of the correct feather for the job is of prime importance. Having selected such a feather, strip away all the base flue and any unwanted fibres, leaving it prepared to the dimensions outlined above. The next job is to tie the wing in, set flat over the back of the lure, whilst at the same time making sure that the spoonlike shape is not lost.

To do this, first position the feather squarely over the back of the lure with the exposed stem slightly further back along the body than it will be when the lure is finished. Now take two or three turns of the tying silk over the bare stem. Do not make them too tight because the stem and some of the fibres are to be drawn under them. Now take hold of the portion of stem that protrudes over the eye of the hook, and pull the feather gently into its correct position with the start of the fibres just becoming trapped under the laps of silk. Done correctly, the fibres caught under the initial laps of silk will enhance the spoonlike shape of the feather, but without splitting their webbed formation. Once you have achieved the desired effect, continue with the silk in firm, butting turns in the direction of the eye. Before the eye is reached, crop away the unwanted stem of the wing feather, and then complete the head in the usual way, finishing off with the whip finish and two coats of cellire.

Mrs Palmer

Richard Walker originally tied this lure up after receiving some pale yellow goat hair, and his expectations that trout would find it attractive in bright conditions towards the end of the season were fully confirmed. He was very insistent that the goat hair be very pale yellow and fine and silky. Bright yellow hair or coarse bucktail were not to be used. He came to regard Mrs Palmer as a deadly killer because it could stand being fished more slowly than any other lure he knew. It is now regarded as one of the very best patterns for fishing cloudy or stained water.

Bob Church has a modified version which employs a tail of white hackle feather fibres and a white chenille body with silver tinsel rib which he uses as an out-and-out attractor in midsummer fished fast. He also regards it as one of the best dirty-water lures.

How to tie

Hook:	L/S 6–8
Silk:	Black

Rib:	Fine oval silver tinsel
Body:	White DF wool with a few turns of arc chrome DF wool just behind the wing and hackle roots
Wing:	Pale yellow goat hair twice the length of the hook
Throat hackle:	White cock hackle fibres tied in as a false hackle
Cheek:	Jungle cock or substitute
Head:	Black tying silk, varnished

Run waxed silk from immediately behind the eye of the hook down the shank in neat, butting turns, and stop opposite the point of the hook. At this position, catch in about 10 cms of fine oval silver tinsel, and then continue down the shank in neat, butting turns, lashing down the tinsel as you go, and stop just before the bend begins. With our very first turn of the tying silk returning up the hook shank, catch in a single ply of white DF wool, and then continue up the shank in firm, touching turns, stopping 5 mms from the rear of the eye. This measurement relates to a size 8 extra long shank hook.

The wool can now be wound up the shank to form an even body. On reaching the anchored silk, tie the wool off with three firm turns of the silk, and then cut away the waste wool. It is always worth a reminder at this juncture that whenever you use light coloured wools and flosses, particularly DF, always cleanse your hands before handling, and only handle the material at its extremities.

The body can now be ribbed with the fine oval tinsel. Make six or seven firm, open spirals over the wool body and, on reaching the anchored silk, tie off and cut away the waste.

The next job is to catch in a single ply of arc chrome DF wool at the position the silk is now anchored. Having done this, wind the silk forward for a few turns, lashing down the raw ends of the two wools and the tinsel as you go. The arc chrome wool can now be wound up to the silk, tied off, and the waste cut away. We are now ready for the beard hackle.

First, turn the hook over in the vice ready to receive the hackle. Now select a large white cock hackle, and strip away from it a fairly generous bunch of fibres, taking care to keep their tips in line. This done, offer the bunch of fibres up, and tie in to form a nice spray around the uppermost part of the hook shank. Now trim away the waste ends of the hackle fibres, and cover their butts with firm turns of the silk. The hook can now be returned to its original position in the vice, and the silk to the head end of the body ready to receive the wing.

For the wing you will require a bunch of pale yellow goat hair which, when tied in, will be equivalent in length to twice that of the overall length of the hook. Cut away a section of hair from the skin, taking care to keep their tips reasonably in line, and tie in on top of the shank. As with most hair wing lures, it is advisable to bed the hair down in a drop of cellire varnish. I usually add this to the cut ends prior to the final lashing down. Capillary action sees to it that the fine varnish is drawn into the hair. After tying the wing in, cropping away the waste hair at a long shallow angle and applying the varnish, the butt ends of the hair are then lashed firmly down with butting turns of the tying silk travelling towards the eye. Any excess varnish squeezed out of the hair by the pressure of the silk should be wiped away, and not allowed to foul the eye. The silk can now be returned to the start of the wing ready to receive the cheeks.

For the cheeks, select two matching jungle cock eye feathers, and strip away the base flue and any superfluous fibres from below the eye. Now position one eye feather on either side of the hair wing, and secure in place with several turns of the silk before snipping away the waste ends of their stems. The rest of the head can now be completed with neat turns of the tying silk covering the raw ends of the jungle cock stems as you go, and finished off just behind the eye of the hook with the usual whip finish. Two coats of cellire will complete the lure.

Muddler Minnow

The Muddler Minnow was designed by Don Gapen to imitate the darter or muddler minnow to be found in the Nipigon River in the United States. Its potential was recognised by Dan Bailey at Livingston who began to tie it commercially, and it became a world-wide success. The dominating feature of the pattern is the deer hair used as head and ruff material, and this is the most difficult part of the fly to tie. How to do so is explained by Bob in the dressing below.

The versatility of the fly makes it a must for every angler's fly box. Even when there are no small fish present, it can be taken for a sedge or a moth or even a damsel. Weighted versions can be fished slowly, sunk deep, but the most common way of fishing it is to retrieve at a slow to medium pace just keeping it on or below the surface. It is particularly effective on the big reservoirs in a good ripple, and when fish are moving in the top layers of the water.

Quality flies always spawn a host of modified or "improved" versions, and this certainly applies to the Muddler Minnow. These include the White Marabou Muddler and other colours, Richard Walker's Texas Rose Muddler which uses orange floss silk for the body and a yellow bucktail wing, the Sculpin Muddler and the Spuddler.

How to tie

Hook:	L/S D/E 6–12
Silk:	Black
Tail:	Two small sections of oak turkey wing quill, matched up and tied in slightly longer than the gape of the hook
Body:	Flat gold tinsel or lurex ribbed with fine gold wire
Wing (Inner):	Sparse brown and white calf tail. Tie the white in first followed by the brown. Extend almost to the tip of the tail
Wing (Outer):	Two large sections of oak turkey wing quill, matched up and tied in to reach to the bend of the hook or just beyond
Head:	Natural deer hair spun onto the shank and clipped to shape
Hackle or Ruff	The unclipped, cream tipped points of the first application of spun deer hair

Run waxed silk from immediately behind the eye of the hook down the shank in neat, butting turns, and stop opposite the point of the hook. Now catch in about 8 cms of fine gold wire, and then continue on down the shank, again in neat, butting turns, lashing down the wire as you go. Stop the silk just before the bend begins. Now cut two identical slips of webbed fibres from a pair of opposing oak turkey or substitute flight feathers, and then match them up by laying them tip on tip, and back to back (concave to concave). The matched slips can now be offered up, and tied in with several pinch and loop lashings to form the tail of the lure. Having secured the tail, the waste ends are trimmed away at as shallow an angle to the shank as possible, and then covered with neat, butting turns of the silk as it is returned back up the shank. Stop the silk after approximately three quarters of the shank has been covered.

Now take a length of medium width flat gold tinsel or lurex, and catch it in by its tip with three or four turns of the silk travelling towards the eye. The tinsel can now be wound down the shank in neat, touching turns until the start of the tail is reached, and then back again in the same manner. On reaching the anchored silk, tie the tinsel off with three firm turns of the silk and cut away the waste tinsel. The gold body is now ribbed with the gold wire in firm, open and equally spaced spirals and, on reaching the silk, tied off and the waste cut away. The butt ends of the tinsel and gold wire are now covered with firm, touching turns of the silk which is then returned to the head end of the gold body ready to receive the first half of the hair underwing.

Select a sparse bunch of white calf tail, and tie it in on top of the shank with firm, forward travelling turns of the silk. Once the hair is secured, trim away the waste ends of the hair, and then cover the butts with further firm turns of the silk. The silk is then returned to the start of the wing ready to receive the second layer of hair. Select another sparse bunch of hair, this time from a brown calf tail, and tie in on top of the first in exactly the same way, after which the silk is again returned to the start of the wing ready to receive the outer wing. Note that the length of the hair wing should extend almost to the tip of the tail, and special attention should be paid to the tightness of the turns of silk which secure it, because this will form the foundation onto which the outer wing and the spun deer head will be tied.

The outer wing of matched oak turkey fibres can now be prepared in exactly the same way as was the tail, and then tied in directly over the top of the hair wing. The length of the outer wing should reach just beyond the bend of the hook, but not quite as far as the tip of the tail. After securing the wing slips, trim away the waste ends at a shallow angle to the shank, and cover the butts with firm turns of the silk. The silk is then returned to within a millimetre or so of the fibre wing, ready to receive the head of spun deer hair.

For the head, select a bunch of natural deer hair, and offer it up for tying in (spinning) with its naturally tapered tips facing towards the bend of the hook. Lower the bunch onto the top of the hook shank, and then take two complete turns of the silk around the deer hair and the shank. Do not make the turns too tight at this point. The silk is now drawn firmly downwards in direct line with the initial turns of the silk. As the silk bites deeper into the hair it will begin to pull it around the shank. Do not let go of the hair at this stage, but hold it less firmly and allow it to flow from your grasp until it has travelled around the shank. Now take two more very firm turns of the silk through the centre of the spun bunch to lock the hair down. This is then followed by one open turn to the right of the last turns to get the silk out of the bunch as it were. The spun fibres are now drawn backwards with the thumb and the first two fingers of the left hand whilst the silk is wound two or three times around the shank as close as possible to the bunch. This will help stack the fibres in an upright position.

A second bunch of deer hair can now be spun on in front of the first in exactly the same way. Then whip finish and cut away the silk. We are now ready to trim the spun hair to shape. Take a sharp pair of scissors and trim the head to a cylindrical shape, taking care not to cut away the naturally tapered hairs to the rear of the head. These should be left to form the hackle or ruff.

Mylar Minnow

Mylar was first used by American fly dressers in the early 1960s, and Tom Saville, the Nottingham tackle dealer, tells me that they were stocking both the mylar tubing and dual-colour strip as early as 1968. The tubing was in immediate demand for bodies of fry imitations as in the Mylar Minnow, a creation of Syd Brock's, one of our top lure specialists and captor of many big fish.

Syd uses the lure in a variety of ways. Firstly, from the bank on a floating line, he will fish it in the top layers slowly and with the odd jerk to attract the fry feeders. Secondly, he will fish it from the bank on a slow sink line near the lake bed with slow, even retrieves varied by the odd pull.

He emphasises that takes are usually registered as something going taut rather than a snatch, and the response has to be quick otherwise the fish let go. The Mylar Minnow is a 'no working parts' type of lure like the Baby Doll so it retains its shape in the water no matter what speed or depth it is being worked.

How to tie

Hook:	L/S D/E 10–14
Silk:	Black
Underbody:	Wool or floss
Body:	Silver or gold mylar piping
Back &	
Tail:	Peacock herl
Head:	Bold head of tying silk, varnished and eye detail added

Run the waxed silk from immediately behind the eye of the hook down the shank in neat, butting turns, and stop approximately opposite the point of the hook. Now take a generous length of fine wool or floss, and catch in at this point by its tip. The silk is then continued down the shank for a few turns, tying down the floss as you go, to finish approximately opposite the barb of the hook or, in other words, just before the bend begins.

The floss silk can now be wound up and down the shank to form a neat, tapered, fishlike underbody, finishing up at the anchored tying silk where it is tied off and the waste floss cut away. Do not take the underbody right up to the eye, but leave at least a 3 mm gap. A length of mylar piping is now cut, and the inner core removed with the aid of a pair of tweezers. The length of piping should be slightly longer than the overall length of the hook.

Having prepared the mylar, push it gently over the eye of the hook and down the floss underbody, allowing the frayed ends to bypass the anchored silk. Once the silk is sitting snuggly alongside the solid part of the braid, the mylar is secured firmly in place with five or six butting turns of the silk travelling in the direction of the bend. Do not allow any of the turns of silk to stray round the bend.

Having secured the mylar, the frayed strands can then be trimmed away as close as possible to the last lap of tying silk, and their raw ends then covered with a further turn or two of the silk. The silk is now left at anchor at this position to be used later to secure the back material.

A new length of waxed silk is now introduced just behind the eye of the hook after first easing the mylar piping slightly back down the body. Do not pull the piping any further back than you have to, otherwise excessive fraying will occur. Once the silk is in place, the piping is pulled taut over the underbody, allowing the frayed ends to pass around the silk as before, and then secured with four or five firm turns of the tying silk travelling in the direction of the eye. The frayed strands of mylar can once again be trimmed away level with the last lap of silk, and their raw butts covered with a further turn or two, after which the silk is returned to the head end of the body ready to receive and tie in the herl back and tail material.

For the back and tail, select a generous bunch (about ten or twelve strands) of peacock herls, taking care to lay them all in the same direction, and tie them in tightly on top of the hook shank close up to the head end of the body. The length of the herls should be long enough to extend from the head to a reasonable distance beyond the end of the finished tail. Make sure that the 'flow' of the flue fibres is inclined backwards towards the tail.

Having secured the herls at the head, trim away their waste ends at a shallow angle to the shank, and form a bold but neat head with the tying silk. The head is then completed with the usual whip finish and the waste silk cut away.

The herls are now laid neatly along the top of the body, and secured at the tail end with four or five very firm turns of the tying silk which is hanging at anchor there. Once the herls are held securely in place, a four or five turn whip finish is performed using a loop which is large enough to encompass the whole of the hook. After the whip finish, trim away the waste silk. All that now remains to complete the lure is to trim the tail to length, and give the whippings two coats of cellire varnish. Eye detail can be added as soon as the varnish has completely hardened off.

Nailer Fly

In its livery of gold, red and brown, the Nailer Fly is ideally suited for high summer trout fishing. As the water warms towards its seasonal peak and visibility is reduced, so oranges, reds and golds become ever more effective colours.

Bob recalls a particularly hard day at this time of the year when he and his partner had not a single fish to show for their efforts on Rutland Water until mid-day. Drifting in the middle of the South Arm and searching his box for inspiration, Bob's gaze alighted on three or four Nailers.

He attached one to the point of his leader and delivered a long line down the wind. After a short pause to allow the slow-sink line to settle in, he began to retrieve with long, medium paced pulls on the line. About halfway back, the line suddenly stopped dead, the rod arced over, but the fish was off. The very next cast brought a large trout to the surface as he lifted off, and the turbulence flattened a huge area of wave. The third time he was lucky, and the next cast secured his first fish of the day, a fat, silver rainbow which was found to be full of daphnia. He finished off that day with five nice rainbows, all of which fell to the Nailer out on open water where there had been no sign whatsoever of feeding trout.

Bob Church uses the Nailer for fishing deeply from a boat on the big reservoirs.

How to tie

Hook:	L/S 6–10
Silk:	Brown or black
Tail:	Scarlet-dyed cock hackle fibres
Body:	Flat gold tinsel or lurex
Rib:	Fine gold wire
Wing:	Two or four scarlet-dyed cock hackles, back to back
Overwing:	Two slips of oak turkey, one on either side of the streamer wing
Hackle:	Chocolate brown or natural brown cock, long in fibre. Make three full turns in front of completed wing

Run waxed silk from immediately behind the eye of the hook down the shank in neat, butting turns, and stop opposite the point of the hook. Now take a large scarlet-dyed cock hackle, and strip away from it a medium sized bunch of fibres, taking care to keep their tips in line. The bunch of fibres can now be offered up, and tied in on top of the shank to form the tail of the lure, and the silk then continued down the shank in neat, touching turns, lashing down the tail fibres as you go. Stop the silk just before the bend begins.

With your very first turn of the tying silk returning up the shank, catch in a short length of gold wire, and then continue up the shank in neat, butting turns to within a short distance from the eye, allowing just enough room for the wing and hackle. Now catch in a length of medium width flat gold tinsel or lurex with two or three firm turns of the silk. The tinsel can then be wound down the shank in neat, touching turns until the start of the tail is reached, and then returned in the same manner back to the tying silk where it is tied off with three firm turns of the silk and the waste tinsel cut away. This is then followed by the gold wire which is wound over the gold body in firm, open and equally spaced spirals until the anchored silk is reached. On reaching the silk, tie the wire down and snip away the waste. The raw ends of the tinsel and wire can now be covered with neat turns of the tying silk which is then returned to the head end of the body ready to receive the wing.

For the wing, select four matching scarlet-dyed cock hackles, and place each pair tip on tip, one on top of the other. The two pairs of matched hackles can then themselves be paired up by placing them tip on tip, back to back (concave to concave). The four feathers are now gripped tightly in this position whilst the unwanted base flue and fibres are stripped away to expose the central stems, at the same time reducing the wing to the required length.

The wing can now be offered up, and tied in by lashing the four exposed stems firmly on top of the hook shank. It is important that the commencement of the wing fibres is positioned in line with the head end of the gold body. Having secured the hackle stems with four or five very firm turns of silk, their waste ends can then be trimmed away at a shallow angle to the shank, and their ends covered with further firm turns of the silk. The silk is then returned to the beginning of the wing fibres ready to receive the overwing.

For the overwing, select two opposing secondary flight feathers of oak turkey or suitable substitute, and cut an identical web of fibres from each. Each web is then offered up separately for tying in by positioning one on each side of the streamer wing with the natural rake or curve of the slip flowing backwards and downwards. Having positioned the two slips to your satisfaction, grip them between finger and thumb, and secure in place with several pinch and loop lashings of the tying silk. The waste butt ends can then be trimmed away, and their cropped butts covered with firm turns of the silk which is then returned to the commencement of the wing ready to receive the hackle.

For the hackle select a large, natural brown cock hackle, and strip away all the base flue and any insignificant fibres. Now offer the hackle up for tying in by trapping the stem close up to the streamer wing, and then making four or five firm turns of the silk travelling towards the eye. Now snip away the waste end of the hackle stem, and attach the pliers to the tip of the hackle. Three full turns of the hackle are now made around the shank of the hook, the hackle tied off and the waste cut away. It is important that this collar hackle has a nice backward rake. This is achieved by stroking the fibres backwards with the fingers and thumb of the left hand whilst several turns of the tying silk are taken over their roots. This done, a neat head is formed with the tying silk and then whip finished. Two coats of cellire will complete the lure.

Pearly

This is a buoyant lure which lure specialist Syd Brock uses in a variety of colours including black, white and orange. The buoyancy largely arises from the pearl or wooden bead secured behind the eye. Syd calls it a water mover because its bulk creates quite some water movement, and so generally it should be fished with a medium or slow retrieve.

The Pearly is a fry imitation and should be fished as such, but Syd has his own special ways of using it. Its buoyancy enables him to fish close into shallows on a sinking line with his White Pearly and a short leader. Alternatively, he will use a long leader and, say, a fast sinker to pull the fly down and allow it to come up again. In the summer months, an Orange or White Pearly can be retrieved on a floating line and 12 foot leader at high speed to attract aggressive rainbows. If you see a bow wave of a pursuing trout, do not slacken your retrieve or attempt to strike prematurely. Generally, the fish will hook itself.

How to tie

Hook:	L/S D/E 8–10
Tail:	Cock hackle fibres of chosen colour
Body:	Wool of same colour tied to within one quarter of an inch of the eye
Wing:	Marabou of the same colour tied up to the eye
Head:	Pearl or wooden bead painted in chosen colour then secured behind the eye with instant glue
Eyes:	Black and white fast drying paint
Colours:	Black, white and orange

Run waxed silk from immediately behind the eye of the hook down the shank in neat, butting turns, and stop opposite the point of the hook. Now take a large cock hackle, dyed to complement the overall colour scheme, and strip away from it a small bunch of fibres, taking care to keep their tips in line. The bunch of fibres can now be offered up and tied in on top of the shank to form the tail of the lure, and the silk then continued down the shank in neat, touching turns, lashing down the tail fibres as you go. Stop the silk just before the bend begins. With your very first turn of the tying silk returning up the shank, catch in 6 or 7 cms of wool, and then continue with the silk up the shank in neat, touching turns, lashing down the butt end of the wool as you go. Stop the silk 2 or 3 mms behind the eye of the hook. The wool body can now be formed by winding the wool up the shank in neat, touching turns, and, on reaching the anchored silk, tied off with three firm turns of the silk and the waste wool snipped away. The raw butt of the wool can now be covered with firm turns of the silk which is then returned to the head end of the body ready to receive the wing.

For the wing, prepare a fairly generous plume of marabou fibres, and tie in on top of the hook shank. The length of the wing should extend slightly beyond the tip of the tail. Having tied the wing in, crop away the waste butt at a shallow angle to the shank, and then cover the raw ends with firm turns of the silk. The silk can now be whip finished and cut away. We are now ready for the head.

Select a wooden or pearl bead of the appropriate colour, and make sure that the hole is large enough to slip snuggly over the eye of the hook and onto the bed of silk that has tied down the wing material. If it is too small, then it must be reamered or drilled to size before proceeding any further. Once the bead has been prepared, apply a coat of instant glue to the prepared bed of tying silk and quickly slip the bead into place. Allow the glue to harden off before adding the eye detail using black and white fast drying paint.

Perch Fry

Coarse fish establish themselves in most reservoirs, and of these perch fry are the favourite prey of trout. Consequently, perch fry imitations are the most popular and profitable patterns to simulate coarse fish fry. From a purist point of view this is imitative fishing. One of the best of the early imitations using marabou was given as early as 1970 by John Veniard. His Perch Fry remains extremely effective, and can be fished later in the season on the bigger reservoirs in the manner of all perch fry imitations.

How to tie

Hook:	L/S 4–6
Silk:	Brown
Tail:	Reddy-brown cock hackle fibres cut to shape
Underbody:	Floss silk, fairly full
Body:	Gold mylar piping marked with a brown felt tipped pen to simulate bars. Alternatively, gold tinsel ribbed with wide brown floss silk

Wing:	Brown marabou feather fibres with one or two orange ones over the top to form a crest
Throat:	Several white marabou feather plumes reaching about two thirds the length of the body
Head:	Black with a yellow eye, black centred

Run waxed silk from immediately behind the eye of the hook down the shank in neat, butting turns, and stop opposite the point. Now select a large reddy-brown cock hackle, and strip away from it a generous bunch of fibres. The bunch is then offered up, and tied in on top of the shank to form the tail of the lure. Tie the fibres in to extend well beyond the finished length of the tail to allow for trimming later on. Having tied the bunch in, continue with the silk down the shank in neat, butting turns, tying down the tail fibres as you go. Stop the silk just before the bend begins. Before we proceed any further, trim the waste ends of the tail fibres flush with the shank of the hook at the point at which they were tied in.

Now take a fairly generous length of floss silk of about 12 to 18 cms, and tie it in a short distance up the shank from the start of the tail. This done, let the silk hang at anchor at this point whilst the tapered underbody of floss silk is formed. To form the underbody, wind the floss silk back and forth, up and down the shank to form a rather full fishlike shape which extends from the point at which the floss was tied in to within 3 or 4 mms of the eye. Make the final winding of the floss finish at the anchored silk to the rear of the shank. On reaching the anchored silk, tie the floss off and cut away the waste.

We are now ready for the gold mylar piping which will form the body. Cut a length of mylar equal in length to that of the overall length of the tapered underbody, and extract the string central core. Having done this, the piping is then carefully slipped over the eye of the hook, along the tapered underbody, coming to rest up against the anchored silk, whereupon it is secured in place with firm turns of the silk. After securing the tail ends of the mylar piping, whip finish the silk and cut it away. The silk is then re-introduced to the shank just behind the eye of the hook, and the head end of the mylar body secured in the same way as was the tail end.

This done, leave the silk at anchor at the head end of the body to receive the throat, and turn the hook over in the vice. For the throat, select a few fibres from a white marabou plume, and tie them in to extend to the point of the hook. After which, return the hook to its original position in the vice. We are now ready for the wing.

138

For the wing, select a fairly generous bunch of brown marabou fibres, and tie them in on top of the hook shank, close up to the head end of the body. This is then followed by four or five orange marabou fibres which are tied in over the top of the brown marabou to form a crest. This done, trim away all the waste fibres' ends, and cover their butts with neat turns of the silk. A bold head can then be formed with the tying silk and whip finished. The tail can now be trimmed to length.

All that now remains to complete the lure is to give the head two coats of cellire varnish, add the eye detail, and the body stripes with the aid of a marker pen.

Pink Panther

This is really a variation on the Tadpole theme, and was invented by Gordon Fraser. Though it will work in any water or weather conditions, Gordon tells me that he tends to use it when conditions are bad or when all else has failed. His favourite time is when it is really bright and water is affected by daphnia or algae blooms. He says that his only secret is to fish it as fast as possible.

Bob recollects seeing Gordon giving a classic demonstration of just how effective the Pink Panther can be, even under the worst possible conditions. The venue was Eye Brook reservoir, the water was like pea soup with green alga, and it was flat calm with bright sun, hardly the recipe for a good bag of trout.

Gordon, who was anchored up close to the draw-off tower, was casting a slow-sink line and Pink Panther towards the dam wall. After a short pause, allowing the line to sink to its required depth, the lure on this occasion was retrieved with long, medium paced draws on the line. When Bob left the area for pastures new, Gordon had already bagged six rainbows!

For some strange reason best known to the trout, some seasons are better "pink" seasons than are others. And as if to confuse things further, there are no real indications as to when this DF shocking pink creation will be at its most deadly. Perhaps the best advice is always to make a point of carrying a few Pink Panthers, and to give them a try when the going gets tough and other tried and tested

How to tie

Hook: L/S 6–10
Silk: White
Tail: Plume of shocking pink DF marabou
Rib: Medium width flat silver tinsel
Body: Shocking pink seal's fur, DF if possible, dubbed and wound on to form a nice tapered body

Run waxed silk from immediately behind the eye of the hook down the shank in neat, butting turns, and stop just before the bend begins. The silk is now returned back up the shank, this time in open spirals, to stop approximately 5 mms from the eye. What we have just formed is a non-slip foundation on which to secure the marabou plume which will form the tail of the lure. Never tie slippery material like marabou directly to a bare hook shank.

Next, prepare a fairly generous plume of shocking pink DF marabou fibres, and tie in on top of the hook shank at the position at which the silk is now anchored. Continue with the silk down the shank in neat, butting turns, lashing down the marabou as you go, and stop when the last lap of the foundation bed of silk is reached. With your very first turn of the tying silk returning up the shank, catch in a short length of medium width flat silver tinsel or a length of number 16 oval silver tinsel. Continue up the shank for a short distance, lashing down the butt end of the tinsel with firm, touching turns of the silk, and then return the silk to the commencement of the tail ready to receive the dubbing material.

The silk is now dubbed, quite generously, with shocking pink (DF if possible) seal's fur, and then wound onto the shank to form a tapered body which comes to a halt just behind the eye of the hook. Once the dubbed body is completed, the ribbing material is then wound up to the anchored silk in five or six firm, open spirals, and, on reaching the silk, is tied off and the waste tinsel cut away. All that remains to finish the lure off is to form a neat head with the silk, whip finish and varnish. One final tip. To enhance the DF properties of the seal's fur, rough the body up a little with the aid of a piece of velcro.

141

Polystickle

Richard Walker's Polystickle which he described as a fly-minnow was a significant landmark in the development of stillwater flies in the post-war era. The "stickle" covered by polythene, a material first mentioned by Ken Sinfoil in *Angling Times*, combined with a back and tail of another new material, raffene, produced an exciting translucence through which the fish "organs" could be seen. Hence "Polystickle". It became known world-wide, and for years everyone had Polystickles in their fly boxes. Then came a new generation of lures, and the old model faded into the background.

Very recently, I was fishing at Chew Valley Lake, and took a 3 lb brown trout in magnificent condition on a Teal, Blue and Silver. It did not even need spooning out; it was cramful of minnows. Holding one in my hand as I browsed through my fly box, I came across a fly that was its spitting image. It was a solitary Polystickle which had reclined there neglected for years. I decided to give it a go though I felt no confidence in it. I cast obliquely from the shore downwind into the area of activity so that the fly was almost static. As I retrieved very slowly, there was a jolting jerk, and a rainbow trout shot off for the middle of the lake, jumping and cartwheeling. The lesson I learned from this is not to lightly discard proven flies in favour of more exciting newcomers.

How to tie

Hook:	L/S D/E silver 6–8
Silk:	Black
Back & tail:	Brown raffene
Body:	Shank ribbed with black silk two thirds of the distance to the eye, then a length of crimson floss silk wound up to the eye. This is then covered and built into a fish-shaped body with polythene strip
Throat hackle:	Hot-orange dyed cock hackle
Head:	Big, bold. Tying silk given several coats of cellire varnish
Eyes:	White and black paint, optional

Introduce the waxed silk to the shank of the hook just before the start of the bend, and lay down a 2 mm bed of neat, touching turns. Now take about 5 cms of brown raffene, and tie in on top of the hook shank, directly over the mini-bed of silk to form the tail and back of the lure. Leave sufficient raffene trailing to the rear of the bend to allow for trimming the tail to length later on. The forward facing portion of raffene is now laid out of the way over the tail, and the silk brought forward and wound up the shank in firm, open and equally spaced turns for two thirds of the distance to the eye. It is at this point that a short length of crimson floss is caught in, and the silk then continued to within 2 mms of the eye. The floss silk is then wound in neat, touching turns up to the anchored silk, whereupon it is tied down and the waste end cut away. We are now ready for the strip of polythene which will form the body.

A 3 mm strip of .003 to .005 inch thick polythene is tied in just behind the eye of the hook, and then wound back and forth, up and down the shank, pulling to stretch it every time the direction of travel is changed at each end of the fish-shaped body you are creating. Once the body has reached the desired shape, the polythene is then tied off at the head end, and the raw end covered with firm turns of the silk. The silk is then returned to the head end of the body ready to receive the beard hackle, and the hook turned over in the vice.

For the beard hackle, select a large, hot-orange dyed cock hackle, and strip away from it a small bunch of fibres, taking care to keep their tips in line. The bunch is then offered up, and tied in to form a short spray of fibres around the uppermost portion of the shank. The waste ends of the hackle fibres are then trimmed away, and their butts covered with firm turns of the silk. The silk is then returned to the head end of the body ready to receive the back material.

Before laying the raffene over the back of the lure, give it a good damping with saliva on both sides. This will make the raffene much softer and easier to stretch. Now take hold of the raffene and stretch it over the back of the lure, securing with several very firm turns of the silk just behind the eye. After cutting away the waste raffene, form a bold head with the tying silk and whip finish. The tail can now be trimmed to length, and then given a fish-tail shape.

Before giving the head two or more coats of cellire varnish, make sure that the raffene and the laps of silk which have been used to secure it are completely dried out. Then, after the varnish has had time to harden off, the eye detail can be added to complete the lure, if you so wish.

Poodle

The Poodle was evolved by John Wadham, one of the Midlands' most successful and thoughtful bank fishermen, and his friends. John tells me that the Poodle they originally used was broadly similar to what is now called a Viva, and that it was tied on a Taylor and Johnson extra long shank 6, now, unfortunately, no longer available.

Most of us lure fishermen have an insatiable desire to move our fly quickly with our left hand, but John, who is a confirmed nymph and small wet fly fisherman, uses the same technique with the Poodle. The presentation, he says, is all-important, and usually consists of a slow figure of eight retrieve on a long leader taking advantage of any ripple. With an off-shore cross wind, the line is allowed to form a large wind belly, and no retrieve is made until it is parallel with the margins. Another deadly method is what he calls the "stop-go" retrieve consisting of one long pull, a three second pause – when most of the takes come as it sinks – then another long pull. The take will often consist of a "going heavy" of the line or a drawing away of the line tip.

What does the Poodle imitate? John says Rutland rainbows took it freely when on shrimps, and browns when on sticklebacks. Bob thinks the undulating action of the black marabou may represent a black leech to the trout. Incidentally, when John leads his Poodles he either places a strip of lead foil along the underside of the hook to ensure they swim the right way up, or lashes lead wire in the head region, covering with the same chenille as used for the body, which makes the lure nose-dive between retrieves.

John has also caught sea trout up to 10 lb on the Poodle from a river full of difficult fish, a roach to $2\frac{1}{2}$ lb, Chub, Dace, a Pike, Perch and a Bream!

How to tie

Hook:	New Partridge S.E.B. lure hook or Partridge Bucktail Streamer hook, size as required
Silk:	Black Naples, waxed
Tail:	Black marabou plume or arctic fox
Tag:	Two or three turns of DRF signal-green fuzz wool between the tail and start of the body, optional
Body:	Black chenille, leaded underbody if required
Body plumes:	Four or five, depending on hook size, black marabou plumes or arctic fox

Run waxed silk from immediately behind the eye of the hook down the shank in neat, butting turns, and stop just before the bend begins. The silk is now returned in firm, open spirals to a position approximately three quarters the way back up the shank. Now select two or three good quality marabou plumes from which the five or six individual plumes will be formed.

The tail plume is the first to be formed, and this will be the largest of all the plumes. Strip away several wads of fibres, and place them tip on tip. When sufficient fibres have been accumulated, they are picked up as a complete bunch and measured up for size against the hook. The bunch is then cropped to the correct length making the cut at the butt ends, leaving the tail ends with a natural taper. The butt ends are now well wetted with saliva and spun between finger and thumb, nice and tightly, in one direction only. This action, done correctly, will produce a shuttlecock formation which will assist greatly in the handling of the marabou. Having formed the tail plume, lay it to one side whilst the four or five back plumes are formed using the same technique. Once all the plumes have been formed, the tying can commence.

First, place the butt end of the tail plume on top of the hook shank directly above the anchored silk. The butt of the plume is now secured on top of the shank with the silk which is then wound down the shank in neat, butting turns, back to the end of the foundation silk, binding down the spun butt of the marabou as you go. With your very first turn of the tying silk returning up the shank, catch in about 6 to 8 cms of DRF signal green fuzz wool, and then wind the silk forward for $2\frac{1}{2}$ mms. The fuzz wool is then wound in butting turns up to the tying silk, tied off and the waste end cut away.

The first of the body plumes can now be tied in. Place the first plume close up to the head end of the DRF tag, and secure in with firm turns of the silk travelling forwards along the shank. The silk is then returned to the commencement of the plume fibres, and about 10 cms of black chenille is tied in by its stripped central core. The silk is then taken forward in firm turns for a distance of approximately 4 mms, and there left to hang at anchor whilst the chenille is wound up to it. On reaching the silk, the chenille is tied off with three firm turns of the silk. Do not cut away the chenille, but simply let it hang at this point ready for the commencement of the next segment of the body. The second body plume can now be tied in in exactly the same way as was the first, after which it is followed by the second segment of the chenille body. And so it goes on in this fashion until the last plume has been secured. The final turns of the chenille which will form the head of the Poodle are tied off and whip finished.

Popping Bug

This American import first caught the public eye when Tom Saville and his friends caught fish on it at Rutland in August 1979. This is a surface-skimming lure par excellence which is fished on a floating line, preferably down wind from anchored boat or bank in short, quick jerks. The concave head, pulled sharply against the resistance of the water, lets off a distinct popping sound, hence the name, and considerable disturbance is created on the surface which may attract fish from far and wide. I am told that they are great fun to fish as the whole operation is very visual and the takes are spectacular.

The heads of the bugs can be painted with enamel or coloured vycoat to add eyes or even more detail. The version Bob describes has a hackle immediately behind the head. A variety of colour schemes can be used.

How to tie

Hook:	L/S 8–10
Tail:	Two large cock hackles, tied convex side to convex

	side, so forming a good vee shape. A large spray of marabou is sometimes used instead of the hackles. Colour to suit the overall theme
Body or head:	Pear-shaped cork, flat or concave at front end. Painted and eyed to suit colour theme
Hackle:	Large cock hackle wound between the cork head and the start of the tail. Colour to suit the overall theme

There is little to be gained by shaping one's own corks for the Popping Bug. Most good dealers will not only carry a stock of various shaped corks, but also the specially shaped hooks to which they should be fitted.

So, having purchased the necessary hooks and corks, the next job is to glue the corks to the hooks. The glue I find to be most useful for this purpose is Araldite Rapid. Once the glue has set, we can then move on to the next stage, that of painting the corks or heads. There are any number of designs and colours that can be used to decorate the heads, so I will leave this to the discretion of the individual tyer.

The actual tying of the Popper mount, which comes next, is the easiest part of the proceedings. Simply run waxed silk from immediately behind the head to a point approximately midway along the shank. Now take two or four large cock hackles, and pair them up tip on tip, convex side to convex side. Whilst gripping the hackles in this position, strip away all the base flue and any unwanted fibres to leave them the correct length for the tail of the lure. The prepared hackles can now be offered up and tied in by their stripped stems on top of the hook shank with firm, forward travelling turns of the tying silk. Having secured the hackle stems, cut away their waste ends, and cover the butts with further firm turns of the silk. The silk is now returned to the commencement of the tail ready to receive the body hackle. Select a long-fibred cock hackle of a colour to suit the general theme of things, and strip away all the base flue and any unwanted fibres, and then tie it in by its stripped stem close up to the start of the tail. The silk is then wound forward to come to rest behind the head in readiness to receive and tie down the body hackle. The hackle can now be wound in close, touching turns up the shank until the silk is reached, whereupon it is tied down and the waste cut away. A whip finish will complete the lure.

Rasputin

The idea of fishing a buoyant lure inert in the surface is a fairly well known strategy these days, but this was not so when Richard Walker introduced us to the Rasputin in his book, *Fly Dressing Innovations* in 1974. It was intended originally to represent a bullhead or Miller's Thumb, but it has been used successfully to take trout feeding on any kind of fry in the surface.

This is the kind of lure where an amateur fly dresser can score heavily as it is unlikely to be available professionally as it is too labour intensive. Richard Walker commended it because it was very light and easy to cast, and because its yielding texture is sufficiently like a real fish to induce the trout to hold on to it.

Although he and Peter Thomas, his boat partner, fished the Rasputin motionless on a floating line, two other methods were also used. The first was to recover it in a series of short tweaks or draw it steadily across the surface. The second was to use a high density fly line and 45 cm leader, thus anchoring it near the bottom and also leaving it without any movement. The takes can be judged by the fact that some of the trout Richard caught at Draycote had swallowed the Rasputin completely!

How to tie

Hook:	L/S R/B 6–8. Partridge bucktail/streamer hooks are ideal
Silk:	Brown
Back & tail:	A slip or bunch of brown mottled turkey fibres
Body:	A rectangular piece of polyethylene foam (plastazote) slit longitudinally halfway through, and then fixed into position around the shank of the hook with a good waterproof adhesive.
Hackle:	An extra large ginger cock hackle, wound on and divided by a figure-of-eight binding. Trim to length to represent the large pectoral fins of a bullhead.

Run the tying silk down the shank of the hook in neat, slightly open turns, and stop a short distance before the bend begins. Now cut a rectangular piece of polyethylene foam (plastazote) away from the main block using a brand new razor blade. The length of the piece of foam should be equivalent to that of the bed of tying silk, less approximately 3 mms to allow for the hackle behind the eye of the hook, and about 7 or 8 mms square. The rectangular piece of foam is then slit centrally along its length about halfway through.

Having prepared the piece of foam, it can now be stuck to the hook shank with its slit facing upwards. The glue I prefer is Araldite Rapid. Mix a little of this glue and work it thoroughly into the slit, and also along the whipped portion of the hook shank. The foam is then slipped onto the shank, wrapped firmly with the silk which has been left to trail at the rear of the shank for this very purpose, and then set aside to allow the glue to set.

When it has set, the body is trimmed to a fat fishlike shape with the aid of a new razor blade. A word of advice, though. When it comes to trimming directly over the slit, the Araldite will play havoc with the razor blade, so what I do is to save all my old blades for this purpose.

Once the body has been shaped to your satisfaction, the tying silk is reintroduced to the shank at the rear of the shaped body, and a 3 mm bed of silk laid down travelling in the direction of the bend. The part of the dressing which will represent the back and tail of the bullhead can now be added.

Take a generous web of mottled turkey feather fibres, and tie it in on top of the shank over the tiny bed of silk we have just laid down so that the natural ends form the tail, then whip finish and cut away the silk.

The tying silk is once again reintroduced to the hook shank, this time just behind the eye, and then wound in neat, butting turns down to the head end of the body. An extra large ginger cock hackle is now prepared and tied in at this position, and then wound on for five or six full turns. After tying the hackle off and trimming away the waste, the hackle fibres are divided into two equal halves on a horizontal plane, and then secured in this position with a figure-of-eight lashing. The two bunches of hackle fibres now lying on either side of the hook shank are intended to simulate the large pectoral fins of a bullhead, so it is with these large fins in mind that we now trim the ends to length. Do not cut the tying silk away at present, but allow it to hang at anchor immediately in front of the pectoral fins.

The forward-facing portion of the web of fibres can now be laid over the back of the body, and secured in front of the fins with several firm turns of the tying silk before trimming away the waste back material at a shallow angle to the shank. All that now remains is to cover the raw butts with firm turns of the silk, form a neat head, whip finish and varnish both the head and the laps of silk which were used to secure the tail.

Red and Black Matuka

Rainbow trout were introduced into New Zealand in the 1880s, and many grew to prodigious proportions. To take these monsters, new styles of flies evolved, foremost of which were the Matukas. Their particular feature consists of two feathers used for wings with fibres stripped from one side of the hackle for the length of the hook shank, and the upright fibres being bound to the shank by the ribbing. The tips of the hackles are left intact to protrude past the hook bend to form a tail.

Surprisingly, they are not as popular in this country as one might expect, but they are favourites of one of our best fly dressers, David Collyer. Apart from the Ace of Spades, David tells me that the Orange and White Matuka is still one of his most killing flies. He fishes it on a floating line with a split shot clipped on to his leader a foot from the fly. The shot makes the leader sink immediately, and pulls the fly downwards which is very attractive to the fish. It is also deadly when cast into the path of a rising fish. The Grey and Red Matuka also still takes its share of fish for him.

Bob gives the dressing for the Red and Black Matuka because this is the one that has done most for me. I particularly remember it taking fish for me at Ladybower Reservoir in atrocious gale and wet conditions one September. They were taken from the bank on a floating shooting head fishing the fly just below the surface with short, sharp pulls. Another fish took as I cast into its rise path.

Though it may sacrifice some wing movement, the matuka has two outstanding qualities. It avoids the annoying habit of long-feathered lures insomuch as the wing feather does not get caught up under the hook, and it moves cleanly and straight through the water.

How to tie

Hook:	L/S 6–10
Silk:	Black
Body:	Red chenille
Rib:	Oval gold tinsel
Wing:	Two black hen hackles back to back, and tied down on top of the body with ribbing tinsel (four hen hackles may be used to create a denser wing)
Head:	Black varnish

Run waxed silk from immediately behind the eye of the hook down the shank in neat, butting turns, and stop opposite the point of the hook. At this position, catch in about 10 cms of fine oval gold tinsel, and then continue with the silk to a position just before the bend begins, lashing down the tinsel as you go. With your very first turn of the tying silk returning up the shank, catch in a length of medium gauge red chenille by its stripped central core, and then continue up the shank, again in neat, butting turns, lashing down the butt of the stripped core as you go. Stop the silk a short distance from the eye of the hook, allowing just enough space to form the head of the finished lure.

The chenille can now be wound along the shank in neat, butting turns, and on reaching the anchored silk, tie off with three firm turns of the silk. Next, cut away the waste chenille, and cover the raw butt end with turns of the tying silk travelling towards the eye. The silk is now returned to the head end of the body ready to receive the wing.

For the wing, select two or four large, matching hen hackles, and align them tip on tip, and back to back. Grip the feathers tightly in this position whilst the base flue and fibres are stripped away to leave the overall length of the hackles exactly right for the finished wing. Having done this, the underside fibres of the wing are then stripped away for a distance which is equivalent to the length of the chenille body, leaving fibres on both sides of the central stem at the tip. This will be the tail of the lure.

The wing can now be offered up for tying in by positioning the uppermost fibres vertically over the back of the body so that the lowest fibres of the tail come level with the rear end of the chenille body. Whilst in this position, secure the wings in place by taking four or five firm turns of the tying silk over the stripped hackle stems at the head end of the lure. This done, let the silk hang at anchor. The tinsel can now be wound back up the body in equal, open spirals, passing it carefully through the crest of hen hackle fibres as you go. On reaching the silk, lash the tinsel down firmly, cutting away the waste and that of the waste hackle stems. The waste hackle stems should be cut away at as shallow an angle to the shank as possible. This will aid in the forming of a neat head without any sudden steps.

All that remains now is to form a neat head with the tying silk, whip finish and apply two coats of cellire black varnish

Roach Streamer

The introduction of the Polystickle and Sinfoil's Fry spawned a host of fish fry and small fish imitations. Though perch fry may be the most common of the coarse fish to be found in the large reservoirs, roach fry are also often present in numbers and figure in the trout's diet. Taff Price has devised a specific streamer imitation for the little roach. It might be described as for the purist lure angler who wishes to fish the fry in the water!

It can be fished in the various ways of fry imitations.

How to tie

Hook:	As required
Tail:	Dyed-red cock hackle fibres with an equal quantity of olive above
Body:	White wool
Rib:	Flat silver tinsel
Wing:	Two white cock hackles flanked by two dark olive hackles

Throat hackle	Dyed-red cock hackle fibres
Shoulder:	Lady Amhurst tippet either side of the wing
Cheek:	Jungle cock or substitute

Run waxed silk from immediately behind the eye of the hook down the shank in neat, butting turns, and stop opposite the point of the hook. Now take a large dyed-red cock hackle, and strip away from it a small bunch of fibres, taking care to keep the tips in line. The bunch of fibres can now be offered up, and tied in on top of the hook shank with two firm turns of the silk. This will form the first half of the tail. For the second half, select a large, olive-dyed cock hackle and repeat the process, tying the olive fibres squarely on top of the red ones, taking care to keep the tips of the two bunches nicely in line. This done, continue with the silk down the shank in neat, butting turns, tying down the tail fibres squarely on top of the shank as you go. Stop the silk just before the bend begins.

With your very first turn of the tying silk returning up the shank, catch in a length of medium width flat silver tinsel, and with your second turn a length of white wool. The silk can now be continued up the shank in neat, butting turns, lashing down the raw ends of the tinsel, wool and tail fibres as you go. Stop the silk a short distance from the eye, allowing just enough space for the wing and throat hackle. The white wool can now be wound up the shank in neat, touching turns to form a nice, even body. On reaching the anchored silk, tie the wool off with three firm turns of the silk, and then cut away the waste. For the ribbing, take hold of the flat silver tinsel, and wind it over the wool body in firm, open and equally spaced turns until the anchored silk is reached. At this point, tie the tinsel off and cut away the waste. The raw ends of the wool and tinsel can now be covered with firm, forward turns of the silk which is then returned to the head end of the body ready to receive the beard hackle.

First, turn the hook over in the vice ready to receive the beard hackle, then select a large, red-dyed cock hackle and strip away from it a fairly generous bunch of fibres, taking care to keep their tips in line. The bunch of fibres is then offered up, and tied in to form a nice spray around the uppermost portion of the hook shank using firm, forward travelling turns of the silk. After four or five turns, trim away the waste butts of the fibres, and then cover the cut ends with further firm turns of the silk which is then returned to the head end of the body ready to receive the wing. The hook can now be returned to its original position in the vice.

For the wing we will require an underwing of two white cock

hackles tied back to back (concave to concave) which is perfectly flanked by two olive-dyed cock hackles of the same size. So, having selected four cock hackles of identical shape and size, pair them up by laying one olive hackle on top of one white one, taking care to align their tips. Having matched up each pair, they themselves can then be paired up by placing them tip on tip, and back to back. The four feathers are now gripped tightly in this position whilst the unwanted base flue and fibres are stripped away to expose the central stems whilst at the same time reducing the wing to the required length. The wing can now be offered up, and tied in by lashing the four exposed stems firmly on top of the hook shank. It is important that the commencement of the wing fibres is positioned in line with the head end of the wool body. Having secured the hackle stems with four or five very firm turns of the silk, their waste ends can then be trimmed away at a shallow angle to the shank, and their ends covered with further firm turns of the silk. The silk can then be returned to the commencement of the wing fibres ready to receive the shoulder feathers.

For the shoulder we will require two identical Lady Amhurst tippet feathers. Having selected the tippet feathers, strip away all the base flue and any unwanted fibres to leave them the correct length for the hook size being tied, and then offer them up for tying in by positioning one on either side of the streamer wing. Hold the tippets in this position, gripping them between finger and thumb, and secure with three or four firm pinch and loop lashings before snipping away the waste stems and covering their butts with firm, neat turns of the silk. The silk is now returned to the commencement of the shoulders, ready to receive the cheeks.

For the cheeks, select two matching jungle cock eye feathers, and strip away all the base flue and any superfluous fibres from below the eye. Now position one eye feather on either side of the Lady Amhurst tippet shoulders, and secure in place with several turns of the silk before snipping away their waste stems. The rest of the head can now be completed with neat turns of the tying silk, covering the raw ends of the jungle cock stems in the process, and finished off just behind the eye of the hook with the usual whip finish. Two coats of cellire will complete the lure.

Ruby

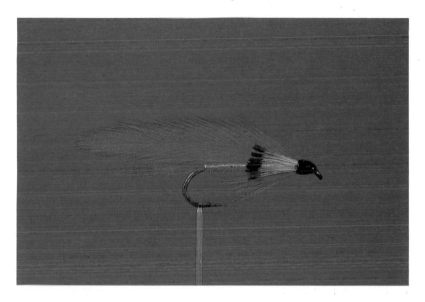

It is worth considering having this lure in your fly box simply because there are very few scarlet or red lures around. It is a creation of Syd Brock, and he says he has had notable results with it when all other lures have failed. He usually fishes it from June onwards on a slow sink line or a sink tip with a leader of 10 to 12 feet retrieved in short, smooth pulls just under the surface. Certainly a lure to produce when fish are getting difficult, and you are looking for something different.

How to tie

Hook:	L/S 6–10
Silk:	Black
Tail:	Scarlet-dyed cock hackle fibres
Body:	Scarlet stretched plastic tape
Throat hackle:	Scarlet-dyed cock hackle fibres
Wing:	Four scarlet-dyed cock hackle feathers
Cheeks:	Golden pheasant tippets

Run waxed silk from immediately behind the eye of the hook down the shank in neat, butting turns, and stop opposite the point of the hook. Now take a large scarlet-dyed cock hackle, and strip away from it a medium sized bunch of fibres, taking care to keep their tips in line. The bunch of fibres can now be offered up and tied in on top of the shank to form the tail of the lure, and the silk then continued down the shank in neat, butting turns, lashing down the tail fibres as you go. Stop the silk just before the bend begins. We are now ready for the plastic strip which will form the body.

Take 6 or 7 cms of scarlet plastic tape, and stick it to a hard, smooth surface. Now, using a straight-edge and scalpel or razor blade, slice away a tapered strip measuring approximately 2 mms at the narrow end and 3 mms at the wide end. Having done this, cut an even finer taper to the last 3 or 4 mms at the narrow end of the strip to assist in the tying in of the strip. Now, with the very first turn of the tying silk returning up the shank, catch in the plastic strip by its tapered end, making sure that the adhesive side of the tape is, at this point, facing away from the hook shank. By doing this, you will ensure that the tape will eventually be wound on to the hook shank with the best side of the tape facing outwards. Continue with the silk up the shank in neat, butting turns, lashing down the butt end of the plastic tape as you go, and stop a short distance from the eye, allowing just enough space for the hackle and the wing.

The plastic strip can now be wound up the shank in barely over-lapping turns, to give a slightly tapered effect to the body, until the anchored silk is reached, whereupon the tape is tied down with three or four very firm turns of the tying silk and the waste then trimmed away. The butt end of the trimmed tape is now covered with firm turns of the silk, and then the silk returned to the head end of the body ready to receive the beard hackle.

First, turn the hook over in the vice. Now select a large scarlet–dyed cock hackle, and strip away from it a fairly generous bunch of fibres, taking care to keep their tips in line. The bunch of fibres is then offered up, and tied in to form a nice spray around the upper-most portion of the hook shank, using firm, forward travelling turns of silk. After four or five turns of the silk, trim away the waste butts of the hackle fibres, and then cover their cut ends with further firm turns of the silk. The silk can then be returned to the commencement of the body, and the hook to its original position in the vice. We are now ready for the wing.

For the wing, select four matching, scarlet-dyed cock hackles, and place each pair tip on tip, one on top of the other. The two pairs of matched hackles can then themselves be paired up by placing them tip on tip, back to back (concave on concave). The four feathers are now gripped tightly in this position whilst all the unwanted base flue and fibres are stripped away to expose their central stems, and at the same time reducing the wing to the required length.

The wing can now be offered up, and tied in by lashing the four exposed stems firmly on top of the hook shank. It is important that the commencement of the wing fibres is positioned immediately above the beginning of the throat hackle, and that the wing lies in line with and at 90 degrees to the shank. Once lashed firmly into position, crop away the waste hackle stems at a shallow angle to the shank, and cover their raw ends with further firm turns of the silk. The silk is now returned to the commencement of the wing ready to receive the cheeks.

For the cheeks, select two small, identically shaped golden pheasant tippet feathers and strip away all the base flue plus any unwanted fibres, to leave the feathers the correct length for the hook size being tied. The tippet feathers can now be offered up for tying in by positioning one on either side of the streamer wing. They are then secured in this position with three or four firm pinch and loop lashings before trimming away their waste stems. The rest of the head can now be completed with neat turns of the tying silk, covering the raw ends of the tippet stems in the process, and then completed with the usual whip finish just behind the eye of the hook. Two coats of cellire varnish will complete the lure.

Scale Fry

This one of Bob's own flies which all began with a box of chocolates. The fancy braiding trimming of the box suggested to Jim Sharpe, the tackle dealer, the small scales of a small fish fry. Bob was asked to see how it could be used and, borrowing the hackle and nice round fuzzy head of a Jersey Herd, the plastic raffia tail and back material of the Polystickle and the chocolate box braiding material for the body, he came up with the Scale Fry which has accounted for countless fish for him and many other trout fishermen since that day in 1967. Unfortunately, the braiding material is no longer available, but the advent of mylar has provided a reasonable substitute.

The lure can be fished in all the usual styles as a fry imitator, but Bob particularly commends two methods where the Scale Fry is unrivalled. The first is as a static lure with a long leader, floating line and single Scale Fry. The angler positions himself upwind of a hot spot, and casts square downwind into the area of greatest activity. In so doing, the wind and ripple will help hold the line over the chosen place rather than drag the fly line around. The takes can come at any time after the cast is made, especially as the Scale Fry drifts enticingly to the bottom. Once it has reached there, you must wait for a "run". This takes some discipline, but Bob assures us that it is a winner on its day.

The other method is for the boat angler using a floating line and more than one Scale Fry. The boat is allowed to drift broadside on to the wind, a short cast made square across the wind and then allowed to swing round and trail behind the boat in a "drift-wake". That is the little whirls and eddies that form directly off the bows and stern behind the boat. The lures are trailed, but only for a few seconds, then the rod is slowly raised and the lure on the top dropper made to skate on the surface, and this usually makes the mind up of a following trout.

How to tie

Hook:	L/S 6–10
Silk:	Black
Body:	The original braid which is much stiffer than mylar is now unfortunately unavailable, but the latter is. Use gold or silver mylar cut to length ·
Back & tail:	Olive-green raffene
Hackle:	Scarlet or crimson with the silver body; orange or hot-orange with the gold body. Wind on and divide on top with the back material
Head:	Bold head of peacock herl

Run waxed silk from immediately behind the eye of the hook down the shank in neat, butting turns, and stop just before the bend begins. Now take a piece of mylar which is the same length as the whipped area of the shank plus the eye. Now remove the central core from the mylar, and then slip the piping over the eye of the hook and down the shank until the anchored silk is reached. The tail end of the mylar is now secured with several firm turns of the silk and, in so doing, has prepared a nice level bed on which to tie the back and tail material.

For the tail and back, take a 5 cm length of olive-green raffene, and tie it in directly over the top of the laps of silk which secured the mylar, leaving sufficient trailing over the rear of the bend to allow for trimming the tail to length later on. Having secured the raffene, whip finish and cut away the silk.

The silk is now reintroduced to the shank immediately behind the eye, and the mylar piping pulled back and down onto the top of the shank whilst at the same time compressing it between finger and thumb. Whilst holding the mylar in this position, wind the silk down the shank, and secure the head end of the piping by passing the tying silk between the finger and thumb grip. Done correctly, the finished body will take on a very fishlike shape, being thin in section with a belly on the underside of the shank. We are now ready for the hackle.

Select a large dyed cock hackle in the colour to suit whichever theme you happen to be tying, and strip away all the base flue and any insignificant fibres. Now offer the hackle up, and tie in close up to the head end of the mylar body. Make three full turns of the hackle before tying off and cutting away the waste. Next, sweep the hackle fibres backwards and cover their roots with several turns of the silk, thus giving the hackle a nice backward rake. The hackle fibres directly on top of the shank can now be snipped away ready to receive the back material.

Before laying the back material over the back of the lure, give it a good damping with saliva on both sides. This will make the raffene much softer and easier to stretch. Now take hold of the raffene, stretch it over the back of the lure, and then secure it just in front of the hackle with three or four firm turns of the silk. Having done this, trim away the waste raffene and cover the butt end with firm turns of the silk. The silk is then returned to the commencement of the hackle ready to receive the peacock herl which will form the head.

For the head, I like to use a single strand of herl, but it is not just any old herl. The herl I use comes from immediately below the eye feather where the flue is at its greatest. Having selected a suitable herl, tie it in close up to the hackle with the flue edge trailing, and the quill edge leading. The herl is then wound on in close turns until the anchored silk is reached, whereupon it is tied off, the waste herl cut away, and the silk whip finished. All that now remains to complete the lure is to trim the tail to length and then shape.

Sinfoil's Fry

Kenneth Sinfoil, formerly head bailiff of Weir Wood Reservoir, was one of the first to appreciate the value of polythene in the construction of the bodies of flies. His Sinfoil's Fry was intended to simulate pin head or young fry, and no better imitation has yet been produced. The very young fry of various coarse fish have very translucent bodies, and the polythene body of this pattern represents this splendidly.

A useful hint from Bob Church is that these tiny fry are very fragile and easily digested by trout so that they do not last for long in their stomachs. If you spoon out a trout, and only find a rather greyish, nasty looking soup, it may well be fry. If you look carefully and discover some little backbones, these will be the remnants of the trout's feast, and confirm that he has indeed been gorging on small fry.

Young fry may be present by late May in the shallows and vicinity of weed beds, and sometimes the glints of the fry themselves can be seen. Fish your lure on a floating line along the shore from the bank or towards it from a boat, remembering that these little fish do not move very quickly and adjusting your retrieve accordingly. Make sure that you carry a full range of sizes from 8 to 14 so that you can match the size of the fry in the water. To emphasise that Sinfoil's Fry remains very effective, a rainbow of 8 lb 12 oz was caught at Bewl Water recently. It was spotted feeding on pin fry near some weedbeds, and took a size 14 Sinfoil's Fry at the first cast! Appropriately, Ken Sinfoil is now head bailiff at Bewl.

How to tie

Hook:	L/S D/E 8–12
Silk:	Black
Underbody:	Flat silver tinsel wound two thirds of the way down the hook shank from the eye, and then back again
Overbody:	A 3 mm wide strip of 250 gauge polythene tied in at the eye, stretched and wound to build up a fish shape
Collar:	Scarlet floss silk. Datam glo-brite is ideal for this purpose
Back:	Strip of brown mallard feather
Head:	Black tying silk, built up and varnished, and white eyes added

Run waxed silk from immediately behind the eye of the hook down the shank in neat, butting turns for 3 mms only. At this point, catch in 7 or 8 cms of flat silver tinsel or lurex, and then wind it down the shank in neat, touching turns for two thirds of its length. The tinsel is then returned back up the shank, again in neat, touching turns and, on reaching the anchored silk, tied off with three firm turns and the waste tinsel cut away. Now take a similar length of 250 gauge polythene which has been sliced away from the main sheet to produce a 3 mm strip, and catch this in with the silk in the same way. The polythene is now stretched, and wound back and forth over the silver underbody to produce a translucent fish-shaped body. Tie off on reaching the anchored silk for the final time, and cut away the waste polythene. The raw butt end of the polythene can then be covered with firm turns of silk. We are now ready for the collar.

Take a short length of scarlet floss silk, just 5 or 6 cms is ample, and catch in at the position of the anchored silk. The floss is then wound down the shank in tight, butting turns until it has travelled about 5 mms from behind the eye, for a size 10 L/S, and then returned back to the tying silk where it is tied off and the waste cut away. Now take a narrow slip of fibres from the "bad" or "poor" side of a bronze mallard feather, and tie in on top of the shank close up to the collar. It is not important to keep the fibres of the slip webbed together. They work better and impart more life into the lure if they are allowed to separate a little. All that remains to complete the dressing is to form a bold head with the tying silk, varnish and add the eye detail.

Spring Minnow

This lure was invented by Bob, and first tried out by him at Muskham Lake in April 1971. Like most of us, he had fished the Baby Doll profitably but, paradoxically, the whiteness which was the secret of its success sometimes under certain conditions of light or the mood of the trout, seemed too stark and merely attracted follows. So, although white would still play a dominant role, he wanted to diminish this by the subtle use of darker materials whilst still aiming for a fry-like appearance.

He finally settled on a tail and back of black plastic raffia, and a body divided into two parts. The first two thirds were built up into a gradual taper with white acetate floss and ribbed through with embossed flat silver tinsel, and the remaining one third of DRF fire-orange fuzz wool. A wound-on white hackle was calculated to lend some movement, adding to the white colour scheme, and a head was devised of black mole fur.

On its first outing, Bob stopped counting at twenty. It wasn't the ultimate lure, of course, but the right lure at the right depth at the right time. Nevertheless, it became a much used pattern by him and his friends to the extent that he began to experiment with different materials to speed up the dressing. The solution was to use three different colours of chenille for the body and head. The first two thirds are now white chenille, the last third DRF fire-orange chenille and the head black chenille. The modified dressing is just as effective as the original.

It has proved a very versatile lure in that it takes fish on every density line you can think of from a floater to a lead core. Though, as its name implies, it is particularly killing in the Spring, using a medium to fast retrieve on a floater or sinker, it can be fished in a variety of ways at other times in the season.

How to tie

Hook:	L/S 6–10
Silk:	Black
Back & tail:	Black raffene
Body:	The first three fifths of the shank DF white chenille followed by one fifth scarlet or crimson chenille
Rib:	Medium width flat or embossed silver tinsel, over the white chenille only
Hackle:	White cock, three full turns, divided on top by the back material
Head:	Black chenille to cover the remaining one fifth of the shank

Run waxed silk from immediately behind the eye of the hook down the shank in neat, butting turns, and stop just before the bend begins. Now take a 5 cm length of black raffene, and tie in on top of the shank to form the tail and back of the lure. Leave sufficient trailing to the rear of the bend to allow for trimming the tail to length later on. Now lift the forward-facing back material, and lay it out of the way over the tail. With your next turn of the silk returning up the shank, catch in a length of medium width flat or embossed silver tinsel, and with your second turn, a length of DF white chenille by its stripped central core. Continue with the silk up the shank in neat, butting turns, lashing down the butt ends of the tinsel and chenille as you go, and stop the silk after three fifths of the shank has been covered.

The chenille is now wound up to the anchored silk in neat, touching turns and, on reaching there, tied off with three firm turns and the waste chenille trimmed away. This is then followed by the tinsel which is wound through the chenille in firm, open and equally spaced spirals. On reaching the silk, tie the tinsel off and cut away the waste. The raw ends of the chenille and tinsel can now be covered with firm turns of the silk which is then returned to the head end of the body ready to receive the DF crimson chenille. Prepare the crimson chenille in the usual way, and then tie it in close up to the body. Take the silk forward for a short distance, and then make three turns of the crimson chenille (equivalent to approximately one fifth of the body length) before tying it off and cutting away the waste. Now for the hackle.

Select a fairly large white cock hackle, and strip away all the base flue and any insignificant fibres. Now offer the hackle up, and tie in close to the crimson chenille. Make three full turns of the hackle before tying off and cutting away the waste. Next, sweep the hackle fibres backwards, and cover their roots with several turns of the silk, giving the hackle a nice backward rake. The hackle fibres directly on top of the shank can now be snipped away ready to receive the back material.

Before laying the raffene over the back of the lure, give it a good damping with saliva on both sides. This will make the raffene much softer and easier to stretch. Now take hold of the raffene, and stretch it over the back of the lure, and secure it just in front of the crimson chenille with three or four firm turns of the silk. Having done this, trim away the waste raffene, and cover the butt end with firm turns of the silk. The silk is then returned to the commencement of the hackle ready to receive the chenille which will form the head. Take a short length of black chenille, prepare and tie in in the usual way, and then wind the silk forward to a position immediately behind the eye of the hook. The black chenille is now wound on to form a neat head and, on reaching the silk, is tied off and the waste cut away. A whip finish will complete the tying of the lure, and all that now remains is to trim the tail to length.

Squirrel and Silver

In September and October, the fry are growing larger, and our imitations must increase in length accordingly. So the order of the day is size 6's and 8's. A very useful lure at this time of the year and in these sizes is John McLellan's Squirrel and Silver. I must confess to a liking for lures using squirrel tail for wings. I like the silhouette they have in the water, and this particular lure has that silvery body and darkish back with the touch of red in the tail, so that when it is moved in the appropriate light conditions it has a very natural look to it.

As its slim profile enables it to sink easily, I find it excellent for probing the correct depth one might find the fish by the countdown method. It can, of course, be fished in the variety of ways one uses for fry imitators. Locating the fry in the first place can be a problem, and a useful tip from Bob Church is to look out for flocks of seagulls congregating in one area constantly diving, in which case they may well be feeding on fish fry.

How to tie

Hook:	L/S 6–10
Silk:	Black
Tail:	Tuft of bright red wool
Body:	Flat silver tinsel or lurex
Rib:	Optional with metal tinsel, but a must if lurex is used
Throat hackle:	Fibres from a silver mallard breast feather
Wing:	Natural grey squirrel tail

Run waxed silk from immediately behind the eye of the hook down the shank in neat, butting turns, and stop when a quarter of the shank has been covered. Now take a length of bright red wool about 4 to $4\frac{1}{2}$ cms in length, and tie it on top of the hook shank by its tip. The silk is now continued down the shank in neat, very firm, butting turns, lashing down the wool as you go. It is important that the wool is drawn tight during the tying down process, and kept in place on top of the shank. Stop the silk just before the bend begins.

With your very first turn of the tying silk returning up the shank, catch in a short length of number 26 silver wire, and then continue with the silk up the shank in neat, butting turns, lashing down the butt end of the wire as you go, and stop a short distance from the eye allowing just enough space for the beard hackle and wing.

A length of about 15 cms of flat silver tinsel or lurex can now be tied in at this point, and then wound down the shank in neat, touching turns until the start of the tail is reached. When you get there, the tinsel is then returned back up the shank, again in neat, touching turns and, on reaching the anchored silk, is tied off and the waste tinsel cut away. The body can now be ribbed. Take hold of the silver wire, and wind it over the silver tinsel body in firm, open and equally spaced turns. On fetching up at the anchored silk, tie the tinsel off and cut away the waste. The raw ends of the tinsel and wire are now covered with firm turns of the silk which is then returned to the head end of the body to receive the beard hackle.

First, turn the hook over in the vice. Now select a large silver mallard breast feather, and strip away from it a small bunch of fibres, taking care to keep the tips together. The bunch is then offered up and tied in to form a nice spray around the uppermost portion of the hook shank. This done, trim away the waste ends of the hackle fibres, and cover their butts with firm turns of the silk. The silk is then returned to the head end of the body, and the hook to its original position in the vice. We are now ready for the wing. The

172

wing of the Squirrel and Silver is identical to that of the Banded Squirrel Bucktail so, in order to avoid lengthy and unnecessary repetition of these instructions, please refer to those paragraphs on page 18 in order to complete the tying of this lure. After the wing and head have been completed, all that remains to be done is to trim the tail to the required length, and flare out its individual fibres with the aid of a dubbing needle.

Streaker

I first became familiar with this lure when reading Syd Brock's section of John Goddard's *Stillwater Flies: how and when to fish them*, and I decided to include it in *Robson's Guide*, my book on stillwater trout flies. I had not fished it at that time, but, after all, there were 346 flies in the book and it was not possible to have had practical experience of them all! Since then, however, it has become quite a favourite of mine with its killing combination of black and orange.

I have found that it will work on both small lakes and big reservoirs. Early this year, it was taking trout on a floating line fished just below the surface at Rockbourne Trout Fishery and Croxley Hall. Generally, a steady retrieve paid dividends. On the other hand, fished slowly and deeply off the dam wall at Hanningfield using an aquasink shooting head in early April, and at the very end of October at Croxley Hall retrieved very slowly on a floater just below the surface, it was equally successful. It also has something in common with a Whisky Fly, and can be operated in the same way in the hot summer months with a very fast retrieve designed to attract the belligerence of rainbows. A really versatile lure, especially in the smaller sizes.

How to tie

Hook:	L/S 6–10
Silk:	Black
Tail:	Black squirrel
Rib:	Silver or white stiff plastic tape, or silver tinsel
Body:	Black plastic strip or black wool
Wing:	Black squirrel tail
Overwing:	Orange cock hackle fibres, tied long
Throat:	Orange cock hackle fibres, tied long

Run waxed silk from immediately behind the eye of the hook down the shank in neat, butting turns, and stop opposite the point. Now take a small bunch of black squirrel hair, and tie it on top of the shank to form the tail of the lure. Continue with the silk down the shank, again in firm, neat, butting turns, tying down the hair as you go. Stop the silk just before the bend begins.

With your very first turn of the silk returning up the shank, catch in a short length of medium width silver or white stiff plastic tape, and, with your second turn, a similar length of black wool or black plastic tape. The silk is then continued up the shank in neat, butting turns, lashing down the butt ends of the wool and silver white tape as you go. Stop the silk a short distance from the eye of the hook, leaving just enough space for the wing and hackle.

The wool is now wound up the shank in neat, butting turns to form the body of the lure. On reaching the silk, tie the wool off with three firm turns and cut away the waste. Now take hold of the silver or white stiff plastic tape, and wind it over the body in firm, open and equally spaced spirals. On reaching the anchored silk, tie the tape off and cut away the waste. The butt ends of the tape and wool can now be covered with firm turns of the tying silk which is then returned to the head end of the body ready to receive the hackle.

First, turn the hook over in the vice. Now select a large, orange-dyed cock hackle, and strip away from it a fairly generous bunch of fibres, taking care to keep their tips in line. The bunch is then offered up and tied in to form a nice spray around the uppermost portion of the shank, after which the waste ends of the fibres are trimmed away, and their butts covered with firm turns of the silk. The length of the hackle for this pattern is slightly longer than most, and should reach almost to the bend of the hook. The hook can now be returned to its original position in the vice, and the silk to the head end of the body ready to receive the wing.

The squirrel tail portion of the wing for the Streaker is identical to that of the Banded Squirrel Bucktail, so, in order to avoid a lengthy and unnecessary repetition of these instructions, please refer to those paragraphs on page 18 for this part of the winging sequence. Once the black squirrel tail wing has been secured, the overwing can then be added, but first make sure that the tying silk is returned to the start of the hair wing.

The bunch of orange cock hackle fibres which is used to form the overwing is selected and gathered in exactly the same way as was that used to form the beard hackle. Having collected the bunch of fibres, offer them up and tie in to lie over the top of the black squirrel hair. After securing the fibres with several firm turns of the tying silk, the waste ends are then cut away at a shallow angle to the shank, and their butts covered with further firm turns of the silk. A bold head is now formed with the tying silk and then whip finished. All that now remains to complete the lure is to give the head two coats of cellire varnish, and add eye detail once the varnish has fully hardened off.

Sweeny Todd

One of the great lures of the sixties, and imaginatively named by Richard Walker, its inventor, the Sweeny Todd. The crimson throat hackle, I believe, is a clue to its name, being an allusion to the "demon barber of Fleet Street", and it has certainly accounted for more "victims" than he ever did.

Bob feels that lures generally speaking fall into three main categories: the specialist group; the seasonal group; and the general purpose group. The Sweeny Todd, without doubt, belongs to the latter group and ranks highly in it.

In the early Spring, it catches trout with remarkable consistency when fished in the deep margins on a sinking line. In middle to late Spring, it can often hold the answer for those infuriating rises to the buzzer when no imitative pattern seems to work, no matter how well it is presented. At times such as these, fished singly on a long leader and floating line through areas in which trout are rising regularly, it can produce take after take while ever the rise lasts. Then, in high Summer as the light begins to go, and the trout leisurely slurp down unseen and mysterious morsels from the surface, if all else has failed to secure a response, then give the Sweeny a try, but for goodness sake do not use too fine a leader (7 lb minimum) because the big brownies which cruise in the higher layers as evening approaches, have a very soft spot for a Sweeny swimming just below the surface.

Then, in the Autumn, when black becomes beautiful to trout on most waters, a Sweeny can be as good a choice as any. The main difficulty is finding the Autumn accumulations of trout, and then the most favourable depth at which to fish which, by the way, is not always that deep.

How to tie

Hook:	Any size from 12 to two tandem size 6's; size 6 and 8 L/S are perhaps the most useful sizes
Body:	Black floss, ribbed with fine oval silver tinsel. Just behind the wing roots two or three turns of magenta DRF wool
Throat hackle:	A false hackle of crimson-dyed cock hackle fibres
Wing:	Black squirrel tail hairs

Run waxed silk from immediately behind the eye of the hook down the shank in neat, butting turns, and stop just before the bend begins. With your very first turn of the tying silk returning up the shank, catch in about 8 to 10 cms of oval silver tinsel, and then continue on up the shank in neat, butting turns, lashing down the butt end of the tinsel as you go. Stop the silk after two thirds of the shank has been covered. We are now ready for the floss which will form the body.

I like to see a flat, slightly tapered body on my Sweeny Todds, and one of the best ways of achieving this is to take a length (about 22 cms for a size 8 long shank) of Pearsall's black marabou floss silk, and separate the two plies. Having done this, take one of the separated strands, and tie it in at the position where the silk is now hanging at anchor. The strand of floss is then wound down the shank, taking care to keep the turns close together at the head end of the body, but gradually opening them out and flattening the floss the further down the shank you progress. On reaching the end of the foundation laps of tying silk, the floss silk is then returned back over itself using the same method to create the desired tapered effect. On reaching the anchored silk, tie the floss off and cut away the waste. The body can now be ribbed. Take hold of the oval tinsel, and wind it over the floss silk body in firm, open and equally spaced turns until the anchored silk is reached, whereupon the tinsel is tied down and the waste end cut away. The raw ends of the floss and tinsel can now be covered with firm turns of the silk, and left at anchor approximately halfway between the head end of the body and the eye of the hook. We are now ready for the DRF magenta wool which will form the final section of the body.

Take a short strand of the DRF wool, and tie it in at the position at which the silk is now anchored. The wool is then unwound a little to flatten it in section as this will help to avoid unnecessary bulk at the winging stage, and wound in neat, touching turns until it just embraces the head end of the body, after which it is returned to the tying silk, tied off and the waste cut away. After covering the raw end of the DRF wool, return the silk to the head end of the body ready to receive the beard hackle.

First, turn the hook over in the vice. Now select a large crimson-dyed cock hackle, and strip away from it a fairly generous bunch of fibres, taking care to keep their tips in line. The bunch of fibres is then offered up, and tied in to form a nice spray around the uppermost portion of the hook shank. After trimming away the waste ends of the hackle fibres, cover their butts with firm turns of the silk, and return the hook to its original position in the vice ready to receive the hair wing. The hair wing for this pattern is prepared and tied in in exactly the same way as was fully described for the Banded Squirrel Bucktail in paragraphs 4, 5 and 6 on page 18. So, to complete the tying for the Sweeny Todd, please refer to these paragraphs.

Undertaker

This has been described as the Baby Doll in mourning, and is one of a number of flies developed from the original. It was devised by D. T. Dale and publicised by Richard Walker. Its inventor fished it successfully on many Midlands lakes and reservoirs using a variety of retrieval rates just like its progenitor. It is, of course, a classic black and silver combination which rarely fails to appeal to trout, especially early in the season.

How to tie

Hook:	L/S 6–10
Silk:	Black
Body:	Black wool
Rib:	Fine oval silver tinsel
Back & tail:	Black wool

The sequence for the tying of this lure is identical to that of the basic Baby Doll on page 12. The only difference is the introduction of the oval silver tinsel at the tail end of the body, and its subsequent ribbing after the body has been formed.

Viva

Victor Furse of Luton created a series of flies all named after Vauxhall cars. The Viva is easily the best known, and the secret of its success seems to lie in its tail. After reading Thomas Clegg's *The Truth About Fluorescents*, Victor concluded that fluorescent or signal-green was the colour most visible to fish, and decided to try a green tail on what was already a successful black lure. The outcome was the Viva. Without the green tail, it bears a strong resemblance to a Black Chenille, but Victor's dressing has a wing of black marabou and black squirrel hair. The original pattern was ribbed with his favourite metallic ribbing to make it sink on the level.

The Viva is an incredibly versatile lure. It is particularly good early season and late, but it will also work at other times. It can be fished slowly and deeply, especially early on, or with a steady retrieve just below the surface. It has taken fish for me at little fisheries like Rockbourne and Croxley Hall, and bigger reservoirs like Ladybower and Siblyback. It can be fished from boat or bank. It took fish consistently for me from Hanningfield in April fished deep on an aquasink shooting head from the dam wall. A characteristic of the takes at this time was that they were quite soft, almost like catching weed or the bottom, so respond at the slightest indication.

How to tie

Hook: L/S D/E 6–10
Silk: Black
Tail: Green fluorescent wool. DRF signal-green fuzz wool is ideal
Rib: Silver tinsel
Body: Black chenille
Wing: A mixture of black marabou and black squirrel hairs. Occasionally one sees cock hackles used for the wing, but the former is the original dressing

Run waxed silk from immediately behind the eye of the hook, down the shank in neat, butting turns, and stop when a quarter of the shank has been covered. Now take six to eight strands of DRF signal-green fuzz wool, depending on the hook size, about 4 to $4\frac{1}{2}$ cms in length, and tie them in by their tips on top of the hook shank. The silk is now continued down the shank in neat, butting turns, lashing down the wool as you go. It is important that the wool is drawn tight during the tying down process, and kept in place on top of the shank. Stop the silk just before the bend begins.

With your very first turn of the tying silk returning up the shank, catch in 6 to 8 cms of medium width silver tinsel, and, with your second turn, a similar length of black chenille by its stripped central core. The silk is then continued on up the shank, again in neat, butting turns, lashing down the butt ends of the tinsel and chenille as you go. Stop the silk a short distance from the eye, allowing just enough space for the wing.

The chenille can now be wound up the shank in touching turns and, on reaching the anchored silk, tied off with three firm turns of the silk, and the waste chenille cut away. This is then followed by the tinsel which is wound over the chenille body in firm, open and equally spaced turns. On reaching the silk, tie the tinsel off and cut away the waste. The butt ends of the tinsel and the chenille are then covered with firm turns of the silk which is then returned to the head end of the body ready to receive the wing. However, before we start the winging process, we must first crop the tail and flare out the individual fibres with the aid of the dubbing needle.

The wing of the Viva is comprised of a mixture of black marabou fibres and black squirrel hairs. The two are firstly intermingled, and then tied in together. Having secured the wing in position on top of the hook shank with several turns of the silk, the waste ends of hair and marabou are cut away at as shallow an angle to the shank as possible, and their raw butts tied down with firm turns of the silk. All that remains now to finish the lure is to form a neat head with the tying silk, whip finish and varnish.

Vulture

This is an unusual pattern because it uses vulturine guinea fowl feathers which have white centres merging to black and with electric blue tips, hence its name the Vulture. Brian Harris, its originator, intended it to simulate roach fry which it did very well with big browns in particular. Brian seldom fishes lures these days, but he still uses the Vulture because it ties in with his current philosophy of imitative fishing. He told me recently that if he used it more, he would add an underwing of white marabou for extra life, the vulturine guinea fowl feathers being a little stiff, so Bob has given a dressing which includes this.

Vulturine guinea fowl feathers had become almost unobtainable, but, happily, Fishermen's Feathers of Crowan in Cornwall are now rearing them specially for the fly tyer. The feathers may seem a little expensive, but Ron Taylor, their director, tells me that the birds cost £350 per pair. The firm, incidentally, breeds other rare birds for their feathers including Jungle Cock, Amhurst and Golden Pheasants.

David Collyer has also used this pattern converted to a matuka style, but Brian tells me that he still prefers the streamer wing because it is more mobile, even though you occasionally experience a hangup of the wing round the hook bend. The Vulture has a very sleek outline through the water, and I usually fish it with a correspondingly smooth and steady retrieve. My Vultures are dressed without the marabou underwing, but I intend to incorporate one and try out Brian's suggestion next season.

How to tie

Hook:	L/S 6–10
Silk:	White
Tail:	A bunch of hot-orange dyed cock hackle fibres
Rib:	Fine oval silver tinsel
Body:	White chenille
Underwing:	Slim plume of white marabou, slightly shorter in length than the overwing
Overwing:	Two vulturine guinea fowl hackle feathers to extend at least the length of the hook behind the bend
Beard hackle:	A bunch of hot-orange dyed cock hackle fibres
Head:	Bold and varnished red

Run waxed silk from immediately behind the eye of the hook down the hook shank in neat, butting turns, and stop opposite the point. Now, from a large, orange-dyed cock hackle feather, strip away a fairly generous bunch of fibres, taking care to keep their tips in line, and then tie in on top of the hook shank to form the tail of the lure. The silk can now be continued down the shank, still using neat, butting turns, tying down the tail fibres as you go. As with all tails, the position should be maintained on top of the hook shank during the tying down, using gentle pressure and guidance with the finger and thumb of the left hand. Stop the silk just before the bend begins.

With your very first turn of the silk returning up the shank, catch in a length of fine oval silver tinsel, and with your second turn, a length of white chenille by its stripped central core. The silk can now be continued up the shank in neat, butting turns, lashing down the butt ends of the tinsel, chenille and tail fibres as you go. Stop the silk a short distance from the eye allowing just enough space for the throat hackle and the wing.

The chenille can now be wound up the shank in neat, butting turns and, on reaching the anchored silk, tied down with three firm turns of the silk. The waste chenille can then be cut away. This is then followed by the oval tinsel which is wound in firm, open and equally spaced spirals. On reaching the anchored silk, tie the tinsel down

186

with three firm turns of the silk, and then cut away the unwanted tinsel. The raw ends of the chenille and tinsel can now be covered with firm turns of the silk which is then returned to the head end of the body ready to receive the beard hackle. The hook is now turned over in the vice.

For the beard hackle, select a large orange-dyed cock hackle, and strip away a very generous bunch of fibres, taking care as always to keep their tips in line. The bunch is then offered up, and tied in to form a nice spray of fibres around the uppermost portion of the shank. This done, cut away the waste ends of the fibres, and cover their butts with firm turns of the tying silk. The hook can now be returned to its original position in the vice, and the silk to the head end of the body ready to receive the wing.

For the underwing, select a slim plume of white marabou fibres, and tie in on top of the hook shank, close up to the head end of the body. The length of the marabou plume should be gauged to be slightly shorter than the proposed overwing. After tying in, trim away the waste ends of the marabou at a shallow angle to the shank, and then cover their butts with firm turns of the silk. The silk can then be returned to the commencement of the underwing ready to receive the overwing.

For the over or outer wing, select two matching vulturine guinea fowl hackle feathers and, if possible, select the narrower feathers as opposed to the broader ones. Having made your selection, place the two feathers tip on tip, back to back (concave on concave). Whilst held in this position, measure them up for length against the hook, and then strip away any unwanted fibres from the base. This done, the two feathers can then be offered up and tied in. Vulturine feathers are very stiff indeed, and lend themselves admirably to being positioned and tied in easily. This in itself is a bonus, because the wing we are about to form should be slightly roof-shaped, and is best achieved if the feathers are tied in separately. So, having prepared the two feathers, take one of them, and offer it up on the far side of the shank so that the stripped stem is positioned slightly to one side of the shank, making the top of the feather "lean over" towards the centre of the hook shank. Secure the stem in this position with two firm turns of the tying silk, and then offer the other feather up in exactly the same way, but this time on the tyer's side of the shank, of course. Once you are satisfied with the positioning of the pair of feathers, they can be whipped permanently into place. This is done by grasping the two feathers between the finger and thumb of the left hand whilst the stripped stems are bound down with firm turns of the silk travelling towards the eye of the hook. Just before the eye is reached, trim away the waste ends of the stems at a shallow angle. The raw ends are now covered with further turns of the silk, a neat, bold head formed with the silk and then whip finished. All that remains to complete the lure is two coats of red varnish to the head.

Wadham's Floating Fry

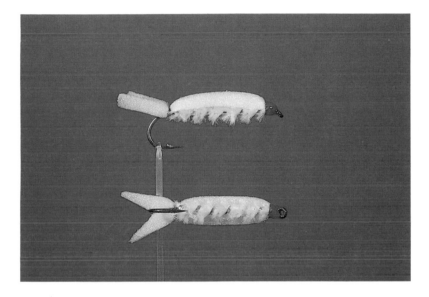

Just as most of us find it very difficult to leave a dry fly out for any length of time on stillwater without the desire to move it, so the same temptation applies to the use of a floating fry imitation. John Wadham, whose floater this is, encountered a gentleman on the point of the Sailing Club bay at Rutland Water who was using an imitation, but having only odd offers. John found it very hard to persuade him that dead fry on which the trout were feeding do not swim very fast! Not only was he not convinced, but he carried on as before. Eventually, he became tired of casting his imitation out and put the rod down. After only a short time, the rod was seen to creep towards the water's edge. He picked it up and landed a 3 lb rainbow which had completely swallowed the lure. The next week John met him leaving the same spot with a limit!

John finds that these floating fry imitations are best fished either directly upwind or downwind. Downwind, however, the fish tend to pick them up and come towards you, whereupon some are missed altogether or come off after a few seconds. Upwind, though, the fish are inclined to take the lure and turn into the wind, thus moving the line and showing that they have picked it up.

John's best catch on this lure was eight fish for 29 lb 10 ozs. This included three 5 lb browns, all taken from a small gap in the weeds in Whitwell Creek.

How to tie

Hook:	L/S D/E 6–10 4X
Silk:	White, red or black
Tail & back:	White ethafoam sheet or plastazote, shaped
Rib:	Medium width flat silver tinsel
Body:	White chenille, DF for preference

To begin with, it is a good idea to prepare several stips of buoyant foam. If you are using ethafoam sheet, simply slice away a parallel 5 mm strip with the aid of a straight edge and razor blade or scalpel. The thickness of the foam should be in the region of $2\frac{1}{2}$ to 3 mms. However, if you choose to use plastazote block, then you must first slice away a length from the main block which will represent the thickness of the finished strips, and then cut it into the required 5 mm widths.

Having prepared your strips, give each one a fishtail effect by cutting a deep vee at one end. Once again, a very sharp razor blade or scalpel is the tool to use for the job. If you are satisfied with the tail effect you have just created, cut the strip into a workable length which, for a longshank size 8, would be approximately 5 cms. Do not be tempted to cut the strips to length before cutting out the vee because, if things go wrong, then the whole piece will have to be scrapped because it will not be long enough. We can now begin the tying.

Run the waxed silk from directly behind the eye of the hook down the shank in neat, butting turns, and stop just before the bend begins. Now take one of the prepared foam strips, and tie it in on top of the hook shank so that the vee'd portion extends for approximately 1 cm to the rear of the turns of silk which bind it. Having secured the foam with five or six very firm turns of the silk, the forward-facing portion of the back material is lifted, and the silk taken to a position immediately in front of it.

With your very first turn of the tying silk travelling back up the shank, catch in a length of medium width flat silver tinsel and, with your second turn, a length of white chenille by its stripped central core. The silk can now be continued up the shank in neat, butting turns, tying down the raw ends of the tinsel and chenille as you go, and stopping about 2 to 3 mms behind the eye.

The chenille is now wound up the shank in neat, touching turns and, on reaching the anchored silk, tied off with three firm turns of the silk, and the waste chenille trimmed away. This is followed by the flat silver tinsel which is wound up the shank in firm, open and equally spaced spirals. On reaching the anchored silk, tie the tinsel off with three or four firm turns of the silk, and then cut away the waste tinsel. Now cover the raw ends of the tinsel and chenille with further firm turns of the silk before returning it to the head end of the body.

All that remains now is to position and secure the foam back material into place. Take hold of the foam strip by its very tip, and draw it quite firmly over the back of the lure, and secure with five or six very firm turns of the silk immediately behind the eye. This done, the excess foam which now extends beyond the eye of the hook can be trimmed away at a long, shallow angle so as to assist in the forming of a neat head. To complete the lure, form a neat head with the tying silk and apply two coats of cellire varnish.

Whisky Fly

This is the inspired creation of Albert Whillock, a casting coach of
distinction. He was a habitué of Hanningfield, and his celebrated fly
was virtually invented for that water. He rarely fished any other lure,
and used to hand out samples of his Whisky Fly in the car park. I
write this in late evening after returning from Hanningfield on a
beautiful Indian summer day in October, and yes, I have brought
home fish taken on a Whisky Fly. Not only does it remain potent
where it first gained fame, but it is recognised as a versatile killer
everywhere, and has reached international renown. More than any
other orange pattern it has provoked enquiry as to why rainbows
sometimes go crazy for that colour.

I took my fish today on a sinking line with a fast retrieve, but
there are times when it will work equally well on a floater. It is most
effective in the latter part of the season, especially on warm, windy
days when algae is suspended high in the water.

How to tie

Hook:	L/S 6–10
Silk:	Orange
Tag or collar:	DRF fire orange nylon floss, shade number five
Rib:	DRF fire orange nylon floss
Body:	Flat silver tinsel, silver lurex or silver Sellotape ribbed over with the DRF and varnished
Wing:	Hot-orange calf's tail or crinkly goat hair
Throat hackle:	Hot-orange cock
Head:	DRF fire orange nylon floss

Run waxed silk from immediately behind the eye of the hook down the shank in neat, butting turns, and stop at a point just before the bend begins. With your first turn of the tying silk returning up the shank catch in a length of DRF fire-orange nylon floss, and then continue with the silk back up the shank, again in neat, butting turns, and stop a short distance from the eye, leaving enough room for the hackle, wing and a generous head.

Next, catch in a length of silver lurex, and wind it down the shank in neat, touching turns to the end of the initial whipping of silk, and then back again to the anchored silk. On reaching the silk, tie the lurex off with three firm turns of the silk, and then cut away the waste. The tag and the ribbing can now be added. Take hold of the DRF floss, and spin it a few times between finger and thumb to tighten the fibres up, then wind on in touching turns to form the tag, after which the turns are opened out into equal spirals to form the ribbing. It may be necessary to keep giving the occasional spin to the floss throughout the winding process to prevent it from spreading. On reaching the anchored silk, tie the floss off, cut away the waste, make a small whip finish and then cut away the tying silk.

The whole body, including the ribbing and the tag, can now be varnished with a clear varnish (cellire or polyurethane) and set aside until perfectly dry. It is as well to make up a batch of bodies at one go well in advance of when they are needed.

Once the varnished body is perfectly dry, the rest of the dressing can be completed. The first job is to reintroduce the tying silk at the head of the lure, and wind it down to the head end of the body ready to receive the throat hackle. Now turn the hook over in the vice, and tie in a fairly generous bunch of hot-orange cock hackle fibres. This done, cut away the waste ends of the hackle fibres, cover their butts with turns of silk, and then return the hook to its original position in the vice.

Next comes the wing. The material I favour most for the Whisky Fly is a nice crinkly goat hair dyed hot-orange. The crinkly hair seems to give the lure added action in the water. Cut away a section of the hair from the skin, taking care to keep the tips reasonably in line, and tie in on top of the shank. As with most hair wing lures, it is advisable to bed the hair down in a drop of cellire varnish. I usually add this to the cut ends prior to the final lashing down. Capillary action sees to it that the fine varnish is drawn into the hair. After tying the wing in, cropping away the waste hair at a long shallow angle and applying the varnish, the butt ends of the hair are then lashed firmly down with butting turns of the tying silk travelling towards the eye. Any excess varnish squeezed out of the hair by the pressure of the silk should be wiped away, and not allowed to foul the eye.

All that remains now is to tie in another length of DRF fire-orange floss, wind on to form a substantial head, whip finish and varnish.

White Lure

Blacks and whites have long been recognised as the killing colours for early and late season, and this is one of our earliest tandem lures, the counterpart to the Black Lure. They are not as popular as they once were, suffering under the disadvantage of the feathers at times tangling around the hook barb, and have been supplanted to some degree in anglers' favour by bucktails, matukas and marabous.

Nevertheless, the White Lure remains very useful, especially if trout are pursuing sticklebacks or fry. David Collyer recommends a strategy of casting to the area of activity, allowing the lure to sink to the bottom – when it may be taken en route – to be followed by a somewhat slow and erratic retrieve building up to a steady pace.

How to tie

Hooks: L/S 6–10, tied in tandem, two or more
Silk: White
Ribs: Fine oval silver tinsel

Bodies:	White floss. Datam glo-brite number 16 white floss is ideal
Wings:	Four large white saddle or neck hackles tied back to back
Hackle:	White cock hackle fibres
Head:	White or black

The tying instructions for the White Lure (tandem) are identical to those already given for the Badger Lure, and it is only the colour of the materials that differ. Therefore, please refer to the Badger Lure on page 15 for the information you may require to tie the White Lure.

White Marabou

This is one of Bob's early season favourites. It utilises the outstanding features of several different types of lure. Bob has taken the tail from a Baby Doll, the white chenille body and flat silver ribbing from his own Spring Minnow, the marabou wing of a Jack Frost and the scarlet beard or false hackle of that old favourite, the Sweeny Todd. The resulting fly is his White Marabou.

Contrary to some views, lure fishing is a skilled occupation depending on a variety of factors such as the choice of fishing location, the use of the prevailing wind, the correct depth at which to fish and the rate of retrieve. When fishing the White Marabou, use a weight forward 8 slow sink from the bank with the wind behind you, if possible, to give your line the opportunity to sink properly. A fast sinker tends to drag up weed on the last half of the journey. Experiment with various retrieval speeds until the most effective one is discovered. In March or April, the deeper marginal areas which have narrow, steeply shelving margins and around ten to fifteen feet of water are Bob's favoured locations. The same water can be fished from a boat, but then a high density line can be used with a weight forward or shooting head. I use an aquasink with yellow stren backing which rarely tangles and can easily be seen. Fish your White Marabou right out to the last few feet as sometimes a trout will follow the lure almost to the surface.

For a darker fly, Bob uses a Black Marabou with DFM red tail, black chenille body ribbed with flat silver tinsel, the wing a generous spray of black marabou and the same scarlet beard.

How to tie

Hook:	L/S 6–12
Silk:	Scarlet
Tail:	White DF wool
Rib:	Medium width flat silver tinsel
Body:	White DF chenille
Hackle:	Scarlet-dyed cock hackle fibres, beard style
Wing:	A generous plume of white marabou

Run waxed silk from immediately behind the eye of the hook down the shank in neat, butting turns, and stop when one quarter of the shank has been covered. Now take two or three, depending on thickness, strands of DF white wool which are half as long again as the length of the hook, and lay them end on end in readiness for tying in. This done, offer the wool up, and tie in on top of the hook by the very tips. The silk can now be continued down the shank in neat, very firm, butting turns, lashing the wool down as you go. It is vital that the wool is drawn tight during the tying down process, and kept in place on top of the shank. Stop the silk just before the bend begins.

With your very first turn of the tying silk returning up the shank, catch in a length of medium width flat silver tinsel, and with your second turn, a length of DF white chenille by its stripped central core. The silk can then be continued up the shank, again in neat, butting turns, lashing down the raw ends of the tinsel and chenille as you go. Stop the silk a short distance from the eye allowing just enough space for the beard hackle and wing.

The chenille can now be wound up the shank in neat, butting turns and, on reaching the anchored silk, tied down with three firm turns of the silk. The waste chenille can then be cut away. This is followed by the silver tinsel which is wound over the chenille body in firm, open and equally spaced spirals as far as the anchored silk. On reaching the silk, tie the tinsel down with three firm turns and cut away the waste.

The raw ends of the chenille and tinsel can now be covered with firm turns of silk which is then returned to the head end of the chenille body ready to receive the beard hackle. However, before turning the hook over in the vice in order to apply the hackle, the tail must first be trimmed to length, and the individual fibres flared out with the aid of the dubbing needle. This done, turn the hook over.

For the throat hackle, select a large, scarlet-dyed cock hackle, and strip away from it a very generous bunch of fibres, taking care to keep their tips in line. The bunch is then offered up, and tied in to form a nice spray around the uppermost portion of the shank. This done, cut away the waste ends of the fibres, and cover their butts with firm turns of the tying silk. The hook can now be returned to its original position in the vice, and the silk to the head end of the body ready to receive the wing.

The wing of the White Marabou consists of one large plume of white marabou fibres, and, if you are able to obtain DF white plumes, so much the better. Having selected your plume, measure it up for length against the hook, and then spin into the shuttlecock formation as described in tying the Cat's Whisker on page 50. The length of the wing should extend from the point of tying in to approximately 1 cm beyond the tip of the tail. This does not include the spun portion of the marabou.

Having prepared the plume, offer it up and tie in on top of the shank, close up to the start of the chenille body. After securing the plume with four or five turns of the silk, crop away the waste at a shallow angle to the shank, and cover the butts with further firm turns of the silk. A firm head can now be formed with the tying silk before whip finishing. Two coats of red cellire varnish will complete the lure.

White Marabou Muddler

It was inevitable that someone would seek to combine the fish-taking propensities of Marabou and Muddler. The outrageously large tandem lure as long as $7\frac{1}{2}$ to 10 cms was invented by Bob Church and Mick Nichols in 1973 to imitate very large fry.

Although not all people fancy the idea of fishing very deep on the big reservoirs like Grafham and Rutland with high density lines, the fact remains that this is where the big fish are often to be found. One of Bob Church's techniques at Grafham is to anchor his boat some thirty yards upwind of the aerator tower where the reservoir bed is some 30 feet down, and to use a lead core shooting head. His advice is that if it does not produce fish at a normal retrieve then the White Marabou Muddler is stripped in very fast. Do not lift your fly out of the water prematurely as fish often follow and take close in to the boat.

The Americans also tie Marabou Muddlers in black, brown, grey, olive and yellow with appropriately coloured wing materials. Single Marabou Muddlers can, of course, be fished in a similar manner to their original Muddler Minnow counterparts.

How to tie

Hooks:	L/S 6–10 tied tandem
Silk:	Black
Body & tail:	White Sirdar brand baby wool
Wings:	Large plumes of white marabou (each hook separately)
Head & ruff:	Natural or white deer hair, spun on and clipped

To give this lure a neater, streamlined effect, I usually remove the eye from the rear hook. The way I do this is to bury the hook deep into the vice with just the eye left protruding. The eye is then gripped with a pair of pliers or forceps, and then cracked smartly backwards.

Now place the prepared hook in the vice in the normal way, and then run waxed silk from a point just before the bend begins, up the shank in neat, butting turns, and stop approximately 1 mm from the end.

Now take two 6 cm lengths of stiff nylon monofilament, and cut a tapered end to each piece. This done, line the tapers up, and lash them on top of the shank, side by side, with three or four turns of the silk travelling back down the shank. The tapered ends should be positioned immediately above the point of the hook. Now take a tube of Superglue, and apply a little along the two strands of monofilament including the three or four lashings of the silk which are holding it in place. The amount of glue applied should be just enough to run between the monofilament strands and onto the hook shank. After applying the glue, quickly continue lashing the monofilament to the top of the shank with firm, butting turns until the end of the monofilament is reached.

At this point, allow the silk to hang at anchor whilst the tail is prepared. For the tail, cut two or three, depending on thickness, short 3 cm lengths of white DF wool, and lay them side by side with their forward facing tips in line with each other. Now take the pieces of wool, and tie them in as one by their tips on top of the shank immediately above the anchored silk. Lash the butt ends down with neat, butting turns of the silk travelling on down the shank, and stop just before the bend begins.

With your very first turn of the tying silk returning up the shank, catch in 7 or 8 cms of white DF wool by its tip, and then continue with the silk on up the shank in neat, butting turns to stop 3 mms before the end is reached. The wool can now be wound up the shank in neat, touching turns to form a nice level body for the lure. On reaching the anchored silk, tie the wool off and cut away the waste.

201

The butt ends of the wool are then covered with firm turns of the tying silk to form a firm and level bed on which the marabou wing can be tied. The silk is then returned to the head end of the body in readiness to receive the wing.

For the wing, select a fairly generous bunch of white marabou fibres, and tie them in on top to the shank, close up to the head end of the body. After securing firmly in place with four or five firm turns of the silk, crop away the waste fibre ends at a shallow angle to the shank, and cover their butts with further firm turns of the silk. Now form a neat head with the silk, whip finish and cut away the silk. All that remains to complete this rear section is to crop the tail to length, and flare out the individual fibres with the aid of the dubbing needle. The head can then be varnished and laid to one side until hardened off.

Once this has taken place, the leading hook can then be placed in the vice ready to continue the tying. Introduce the silk to the shank immediately behind the eye of the hook, and then run it down the shank in neat, butting turns to a point just before the bend begins, and there let it hang at anchor. Now take hold of the rear section of the lure, and offer the monofilament strands up for tying in. Position the strands so that they lie side by side on top of the shank, and then secure them there with four or five firm turns of the silk. It is important that the head end of the rear hook is correctly positioned at this point. Once secured in this position, the Superglue can then be applied in exactly the same way as it was for the rear hook. As soon as the glue has been applied, the silk is wound up the shank in neat, butting turns, lashing down the monofilament as you go. Stop the silk when approximately two thirds of the shank has been covered, and then crop the excess monofilament strands away close up to the last laps of silk at a shallow angle to the shank.

Now prepare a tail in exactly the same way as you did for the rear hook, and then tie it in on top of the hook shank by its tips at the position of the silk, namely at the two thirds mark on the shank. The silk is now taken back down the shank in neat, butting turns, lashing the tail material down on top of the shank as you go. Stop just before the bend begins. With your very first turn of the tying silk returning up the shank, catch in a length of white DF wool by its tip, and then continue on up the shank in neat, butting turns, lashing down the raw end of the wool as you go, and stop on reaching the ends of the monofilament. The wool can now be wound along the shank to form the body in exactly the same way as we did for the rear hook and, on reaching the anchored silk, tied off and the waste cut away. As before, cover the butt ends of the cropped wool with firm turns of the silk to form a firm and level bed for the wing and the head.

The front wing can now be prepared, and tied in in exactly the same way as was the rear wing. After cropping away the waste ends and covering their butts with firm turns of the silk, the silk is then returned to the head end of the body ready to receive the head of spun deer hair. Note that the rear wing is slightly longer than the tail whilst the front wing has to come level with the tips of the rear wing.

The head and ruff of this lure are formed in precisely the same manner as for the Muddler Minnow so, in order to avoid lengthy and unnecessary repetition, please turn to page 124.

Yellow Fellow

This is a gaudy streamer fly invented by David Collyer which has something in common with his Haymaker. The prevalence of rainbows in our waters has led to the introduction of a great deal more colour and flash into our lures, and yellow can score on its day on two counts. Firstly it is a very visible colour and can be seen well in murky or pea soup conditions. One day when I was fishing Chew Valley Lake recently from the south shore with a brisk north westerly and dark clouds the water was almost grey, and only bright yellows and hot-oranges caught the trout's eyes. I understand from David Collyer that he still finds Yellow Fellow successful in these circumstances.

Secondly, the lure can be used on those hot midsummer days – not that there were many this year – to retrieve quickly on a floating line and long leader just below the surface hopefully to attract the angry or curious intentions of a marauding rainbow. It is one of the most exciting aspects of fly fishing to see that following bow wave, and one I would not want to miss, but for less experienced fishermen tempted to strike too soon, David's advice to close your eyes, keep retrieving and open them again after you find the fish has hooked itself, is well worth trying.

How to tie

Hook:	L/S 10
Silk:	Yellow
Tail:	White baby wool
Body:	Silver tinsel or lurex
Rib:	Optional with metal silver tinsel, but a must if lurex is used
Wing:	Four slim, bright yellow cock hackles
Hackles:	Rear, well marked badger cock; front, short fibred yellow cock

Run waxed silk from immediately behind the eye of the hook down the shank in neat, butting turns for about 4 cms. Now take a single strand of white baby wool, and tie it in by its tip on top of the hook shank to trail well beyond the bend of the hook. Continue with the silk down the shank in neat, butting turns, pulling the wool taut and lashing it to the top of the shank as you go. Stop the silk just before the bend begins.

With your very first turn of the silk returning up the shank, catch in about 8 cms of fine silver wire, and then continue up the shank with the silk in neat, butting turns, lashing down the butt end of the silver wire as you go. Stop the silk a short distance from the eye of the hook, allowing just enough space for the wing and two wound-on hackles. It is at this point that we now catch in about 15 cms of medium width flat silver tinsel or lurex with three or four turns of the silk. Having done this, the tinsel is now wound down the shank in neat, touching turns until the start of the tail is reached, and then back again to the anchored tying silk in the same manner. On reaching the silk, tie the tinsel off with three firm turns, and then snip away the waste tinsel. This is now followed by the ribbing wire which is wound over the silver tinsel or lurex body in firm, open and equally spaced spirals until the anchored silk is reached. On fetching up there, tie the wire down and snip away the waste. The raw ends of the tinsel and wire can now be covered with neat turns of the tying silk which is then returned to the head end of the body ready to receive the wing. Crop the tail to length and flair out the individual fibres with the aid of a dubbing needle.

For the wing, select four slim, bright yellow cock hackles, and place each pair tip on tip, one on top of the other. The two pairs of matched hackles can then themselves be paired up by placing them tip on tip, back to back (concave on concave). The four feathers are now gripped tightly in this position whilst the base flue and fibres are stripped away to leave the overall length of the hackles exactly right for the finished wing. The wing can now be offered up, and tied in by lashing the four exposed stems firmly on top of the hook shank. It is important that the commencement of the wing fibres is positioned in line with the head end of the tinsel body. Having secured the hackle stems with four or five very firm turns of the silk, their waste ends can then be trimmed away at a shallow angle to the shank and their ends covered with further firm turns of the silk. The silk can then be returned to the commencement of the wing fibres ready to receive the first of the two hackles.

For the first hackle, select a well marked badger cock, and prepare by stripping away all the base flue and any insignificant fibres. The length of the hackle fibres should reach from the point of tying in almost to the point of the hook. Having prepared the hackle, tie it in by its stripped stem, close up to the start of the wing. Make three full turns of the hackle, then tie off and trim away the waste end. Now sweep the hackle fibres backwards with the finger and thumb of the left hand, and then cover their roots with several turns of the silk. This will give the hackle a nice backward slant. The second hackle, a bright yellow cock that is slightly shorter in the fibre, can now be selected, prepared and tied in in exactly the same way as was the first. As before, make three full turns with this second hackle before tying off and trimming away the waste. This time, however, the slant of the finished hackle should be slightly less than that of the first. Finish the lure off by forming a neat head with the tying silk, whip finish and varnish.

Zonker

Al Troth, the well known American fly tyer, first wrote about his modified Zonker in the magazine, *Fly Tyer*, in November 1981. Fur strip wings have been around a long time, especially in New Zealand and Australia, but the original Zonker pattern was created in Colorado by Dan Byford. His dressing had a loose mylar tubing body. What Al Troth did was to give it a "belly" by using a material called Trimbrite, a thin aluminium sheeting with an adhesive on one side. Our Zonkers use Georeflective strip to achieve the same effect.

The Zonker lends itself to being fished at any water level. The rabbit fur is quite resistant to becoming saturated with water, so that, with a few false casts, it will remain buoyant enough to float, whilst a degreased leader will enable it to be retrieved just below the surface. Al Troth inserted a piece of strip lead between the tape that forms the belly section if he wanted the fly to fish more deeply.

Al Troth described using the Zonker on rivers, but Steve Parton tells me that it has been used extensively on the Great Lakes and other major impoundments. Bev Harper Smith first tried it out successfully at Roger Daltry's Lakedown using deep tactics and a slow sink line.

There are times when mylar is a frustrating material to use, and if you have lack of success, it is worth trying building up a similar type of body using the new Bobby Dazzle material which is so much easier to work. The silver and gold are just as attractive and effective as mylar.

How to tie

Hook:	L/S nickel 2–6
Silk:	Red
Body:	Mylar piping, silver or gold, one eighth or three sixteenths diameter
Underbody:	Georeflective strip
Wing:	Rabbit fur strip on hide
Coating:	Clear epoxy

The Zonker can be tied with or without an underbody "former" of Georeflective strip. If the strip is omitted, the actual tying in of the mylar piping is exactly the same as if it had been used, but an effort should be made to give the body a certain amount of shape and depth.

So let us start off by attaching and then shaping the Georeflective strip which will give the finished body its shape and firmness. From the main sheet of material, from now on GRM, cut away an oblong of, say, 27 mms by 10 mms which would be ideal for an average size 4 4X longshank hook. The length we are aiming for, no matter what the hook size, should be a little shorter than the body length, namely the straight portion of the hook shank. The width should be approximately twice that of the gape of the hook on which we are working.

The next job is to remove the peel-off protective paper from the back of the small oblong of GRM we have just prepared. This done, place the strip centrally, sticky side down, on top of the hook shank. Position the strip so that it lies 3 mms behind the eye and 3 mms from the start of the bend. This is to allow ample space for the laps of silk which will eventually secure the mylar, rabbit's fur back and the throat hackle.

Once in place, fold the strip under the shank until both of the sticky faces come together. The hook is then laid on a flat, firm surface, and both sides of the GRM strip rubbed firmly together using the smooth, flat handle of a tea spoon or similar. Whilst rubbing the two faces together, pay special attention to working in close and firmly along both sides of the shank. This will help to prevent the underbody from pivoting on the shank.

Having fixed the strip firmly in place, it can be cut to the desired shape. This operation can be carried out by using either sharp, fine-pointed scissors or a very fine pointed scalpel. If a scalpel is used, the hook is laid on a firm, flat surface, preferably covered with a sheet of thick cardboard, and then, holding the scalpel rather like a pen, the body is cut to shape freehand. Whatever you do, make sure not to be too generous with the depth of the body (belly), otherwise it may mask the point enough to impede its hooking qualities.

We can now proceed with the mylar body. Take a length of mylar, and cut away a portion long enough to overhang the bend by $1\frac{1}{2}$ cms and the eye by 5 mms (for a size 4 4X longshank this would be approximately $5\frac{1}{2}$ cms). The next job is to remove the central string core from the piping with the aid of a pair of tweezers, and then unravel and flare out approximately 2 cms of the braid at the tail end of the piping using the point of the dubbing needle.

The silk can now be introduced to the shank just before the bend, and then wound firmly up the shank in neat, butting turns until two or three turns have just trapped the tapered end of the GRM underbody. Now take the prepared piece of mylar and pass it over the eye of the hook and down the shaped underbody, not stopping until the silk has passed through the flared out strands, and come to rest up against the solid braid of piping.

Once this stage is reached, the tail end loose strands of mylar are held in place with the finger and thumb of the left hand, whilst five or six very firm, neat, butting turns of the tying silk are made, travelling in the direction of the bend. Now, for extra security, so that these lashings do not work loose, make a four or five turn whip finish over the original whippings, pull tight and then allow the silk to hang at anchor until it is next required. Now to secure the forward end of the mylar.

First wax a new length of silk, and then introduce it to the shank just behind the eye by pulling the mylar piping back down the shank and out of the way. Wind the silk in neat, butting turns down the shank until two or three laps have covered the start of the GRM underbody. The action of drawing the mylar over the broad under-body will cause the ends to become unwound and open, similar to when we picked them out with the dubbing needle for the tail, but to a slightly lesser degree.

The mylar can now be eased forward again, and drawn tightly over the underbody "former" and, in so doing, passing the splayed out ends either side of the silk in exactly the same way as we did for the tail. The mylar is then secured in place with firm turns of the silk travelling in the direction of the eye. Stop the silk a short distance from the eye, and trim away all the waste ends of mylar as close as possible to the last lap of silk. The silk can now be returned to the head end of the body and the tail trimmed to size.

Next, cut a strip of rabbit's skin complete with fur, as described in the tying of the Blithfield Rabbit on page 38, which is slightly longer than the overall length of the hook plus tail. This is then offered up, and tied in on top of the shank, close up to the head end of the body. After securing with four or five firm turns of the silk, cut away the waste hide, and then turn the hook over in the vice ready to receive the hackle.

For the beard hackle, select a large grizzle cock hackle, and strip away a generous bunch of fibres, taking care to keep their tips in line. The bunch is then offered up, and tied in to form a nice spray around the uppermost portion of the hook shank using firm, forward turns of the silk. After four or five turns, trim away the waste ends of the fibres and cover their raw butts with further firm turns of the silk. The hook can then be returned to its original position in the vice, a neat head formed with the tying silk, whip finished and the silk cut away.

We are now ready for the final stage which is that of securing the strip of fur at a position just before the bend begins. Start by laying the strip of fur along the top of the body (shank), stretching it quite tightly. Then, at a point immediately above the anchored silk (which was used to secure the tail end of the mylar), part the fur by stroking it forwards to the head. This is to make way for the laps of silk which will be used to secure it in this position. The silk is how taken around the shank, firmly trapping the strip into place. There then follow four or five more very firm turns of the silk travelling in the direction of the bend, after which a four or five turn whip finish is performed in the opposite direction using a loop which is large enough to encompass the whole of the hook.

After pulling the whip finish tight, cut away the waste silk, and trim the excess hide (not fur and hide) level with the mylar tail. All that now remains is to red varnish both the head and the tail whippings.